Home on the V̶ANDEVERT R̶ANCH

WHERE THE SKIES WERE NOT CLOUDY ALL DAY

Grace Vandevert McNellis

D0707377

RED APPLE
PUBLISHING
GIG HARBOR, WASHINGTON

FIRST EDITION

RED APPLE PUBLISHING
15010 113th St. KPN
Gig Harbor, WA 98329-5014
(253) 884-1450

Printed by Gorham Printing
Rochester, WA 98579

ISBN 1-880222-40-X

Library of Congress Catalog Card Number 99-76235

The cover photo is of Grace and her brother Claude in front of the
ranch house. On the porch is their father (circa 1933).

Cover design by Carol W. Gardner, present owner of the Vandevert
Ranch, and Amy McCroskey.

Dedication

This book is dedicated to my five wonderful sons—Tom, Mike, John, Steve, and Joe. They were lucky enough to know the Vandevert Ranch, their Grandfather Claude and Grandma Jeanie, and to speak of them often. I wanted them to have an idea of what it was like to grow up in that era before modern conveniences and what a different pace life was at that time. They will learn things that I have forgotten to tell them, and I'm sure they will be surprised that their mother did some of those things.

The Old Homestead, circa 1927

The Ranch in the Wintertime

Acknowledgments

I wish to thank . . .

MY BROTHER CLAUDE for helping me with some of the facts that had eluded me and for encouraging me to "keep going" with the story.

MY FRIEND, BERT HAGEN, in Bend, Oregon, who was the one who inspired me to write my story long before I ever thought of doing so.

A few of those with other kind words—CAROL GARDNER, BOB AND JOAN ORR, KEITH CLARK, FRED PURSLEY.

Thank you all for taking the time to read and push me to go ahead! Without this extra confidence you all gave me, the book would still be unwritten.

L-R: Barbara, Claude, and Grace in front of ranch house.

Table of Contents

Introduction

This journal was written in late 1998 with a great deal of work and memory search. It has been a labor of love in looking back at those days when I was growing up in an atmosphere of love and caring. I was so lucky to have a large, wonderful family of aunts, uncles, cousins, and grandfathers around me . . . along with my own immediate family of Dad, Mother, Claude, Mary Jean, and Dave.

I wanted to try to put down on paper some of the events of my life as a child and young girl on the Vandevert Ranch to leave to my sons and families. They have heard me talk about it a great deal, and I would like my family to know why I loved it so much.

I was born and raised on this cattle ranch just south of Bend, Oregon, on the Fourth of July, 1929, and lived there during the years before World War II and for a short time after.

I tell of my schooling in the small, one-room schoolhouse located on the ranch, then in LaPine, and finally in Bend in 1947.

There were the good times and the bad times—not really "bad" but difficult—times when it was too cold to go outside—other times when it was so hot that we "lived" in the Little Deschutes River right outside our door—and times when ranching was hard. In reminiscing, we usually remember the good times and keep the others in a corner someplace to only be brought out, if necessary, at a later time.

I believe this was a unique time in this century, and I wanted to leave my memories of what life was like in my early days. Those were days before electricity, running water, television, credit cards, saran wrap, fast foods, and many other things that are taken for granted today. I wanted people to know, in the future, what that life was like. I feel so privileged to have been raised there and wish that every child could have had just a taste of that life that I loved.

—GVM

The Beginning of an Era—1892

My parents, Claude and Pearl

My mother's family from left: Daniel Catlow, Harry, Charles, Frank, Wilbur (baby), and Melissa Catlow

My Parents

My parents were Claude Chandler Vandevert and Pearl Marie Catlow Vandevert. My grandparents were W. P. Vandevert and Sadie Vincentheller Vandevert on my father's side and Dan and Melissa Peters Catlow on my mother's side. My father's family came to Oregon in 1892, and there is a book about that era and how the family ended up in Central Oregon. My mother's family originally came from Iowa and then went west to Portland, Oregon, in the early 1900s. I knew both grandfathers, but my two grandmothers died before I was born.

My Mother's Family—The Catlows

My mother was born in Atlantic, Iowa. Her mother's name was Melissa Ann Peters. Melissa's father and mother were Jerome Napoleon Peters and Sara Maria France. The father of Jerome Peters was Christian Peters, who married Susan Moats in 1822. Christian was born in Baden-Baden, Germany. Grandmother Melissa had seven siblings, and they lived in Clayton and Cass County, Iowa. Melissa Peters married Daniel Catlow in Bear Grove Township (near Atlantic), Iowa, on March 13, 1884. They lived in Atlantic, Iowa, where my mother was born. My mother had four brothers—all older! People always asked her if she didn't wish she had a sister—and she always said, "No, I'd just like to have four more brothers like these!" What is so funny is that she got her wish when she married my father. He had four brothers, and she loved each and every one as dearly as they loved her. She grew up in Portland, went to Franklin High School, was in school plays—played in *Pirates of Penzance*—and was a good student. I have some notebooks that she kept from those days. She also had a large collection of books given to her over the years that she brought to the ranch after marriage.

My grampa, Daniel Catlow, was born in Burnley, Lancashire, England, on November 8, 1857. I show that he had four brothers and one sister—all born in England. When they came to America, they settled in Cook County, Illinois, and eventually in Bear Grove Township, Cass County, Iowa. That is where my mother and her four brothers were born. I know that my Grampa Catlow worked at a number of things in Portland, some of which involved interior painting and decorating some of the fine homes in the hills of Portland. He was noted for that work.

He also worked on the Crooked River Bridge (train bridge) along with his sons in later years. I only found this out recently, and here we had driven over the bridge next to it all these years on the way to the ranch! My sons saw it when they were small, and I expect they still stop there to look down in that deep canyon just before they get to Redmond on the way in to Bend. Grampa Catlow lost his wife on May 4, 1924, in Portland. I have some of her letters to one of her sisters back in Iowa. I also have a pink baby quilt with Mother Goose characters on it that she made for my mother, Pearl, when she was to have a baby at the ranch. She tells about it in one of her letters. I had never known where the quilt came from until I found this letter. I know that she came to the ranch several times to be with my mother, and my Grampa Catlow would miss her very much. I have letters that relate to that time too. I always wished that I had known her. She had the sweetest face in her pictures and looked like she would have been a wonderful grandma!

My Mother's Brothers

My mother's brothers were Charles, Frank, Harry and Wilbur Catlow. Uncle Charlie worked for the Union Pacific Railroad in Portland when I knew him. He was married to Edna Bell and they had two sons, Albert and Charlie. My Aunt Edna was also the Grand Guardian of Oregon for Job's Daughters and the past Grand Secretary of Job's Daughters at one time. She and Uncle Charlie were very active in the Eastern Star. Their family would come to the ranch each year. Uncle Charlie would fish in the river all day if we let him. Aunt Edna would help my mother with whatever was going on. The boys either played or worked with Claude and did the things all young fellows do. They were a little older than I was, so I didn't get to run around with them very much! I got in the way! But whenever I went to Portland, I got to stay with them, and they treated me like a queen! They had a lovely old home where my Grampa Catlow lived with them until his death in 1934. My mother and I took a bus to Portland for the funeral. I didn't go to the funeral itself—can't remember where I stayed during that day.

L-R: Frank, (Pearl), Charlie, Harry

When we got to Portland, I can remember hoping the Easter bunny could find me! It was Easter weekend, and I was sure he would come to the ranch, and when he couldn't find my basket, he would leave! Well, that was all taken care of by the Portland Easter bunny! When I awoke on Easter Sunday, here was a whole box of Easter eggs and candies with my name on it! Somehow, he knew where I was! I was very impressed and happy! Also, this was the time that my Uncle Charlie and Aunt Edna told me about how they got their milk in Portland. They said that every morning a cow came down the street and a man would just milk the cow right into the bottles that were on the front porch! Well, I was very intrigued to see this cow! I went out to the front porch and sat up on an overhanging railing waiting. All of sudden, I fell off—down I went into the flowers! The family came and got me and took me into the house to recover and, as soon as I could, I went back out to wait for the cow! However, while I was inside, that darned cow had come and gone and I never did get to see her! I was very disappointed! I always wondered why my dad laughed so much at the story I brought back from Portland!

Uncle Frank was married to Aunt Bertha. He was my "funny" uncle—always laughing and having a wonderful smile on his face. They had just one daughter, Elizabeth, who passed away in the early 1990s. Uncle Frank was kind of a jack-of-all-trades. I know that he, his father, and brother Harry worked on the Crooked River Gorge Railroad Bridge that is still there just outside Redmond. I have pictures of them from the Redmond area where they would live during the summer and kind of "camp out." Sometimes, their mother would join them from Portland. I don't have details as to how long they worked there, but it was quite some time. Uncle Frank could build anything. He also had a cabin at the ocean where they went a great deal of the time. He loved to fish and garden, and we loved having him come to the ranch.

I only remember Uncle Harry a little bit. He took me to the zoo in Portland when I was very small and, at the time, the zoo was not in great shape. He took me into this big building and there were monkeys, which I had never seen before. Then he took me over to a cage and said, "Look at this fellow!" It was a blue-faced baboon and it scared me to death! I thought it was the ugliest thing I had ever seen! I will never, ever, forget it! Uncle Harry also took me all around on streetcars, elevators, escalators, and all the things that I had never been on before. We just didn't have anything like that in Bend! They had two children, a boy, William, whom we called "Little Bill," and a girl, Alice. I barely remember either of them—really only Bill. He loved to swim at the ranch, and I have a picture of him sitting on the diving board down at the river. I believe he is dead now and I believe Alice is too. I know nothing of their families.

Uncle Wilbur was a soldier during World War I and fought in France. There are stories about those times in some of my mother's papers. He managed to get home after the war but died a short time later from the after effects of poison gas used in that awful war. He was the youngest of my mother's brothers, and they were very close. I have lots of pictures of them taken in studios, just the two of them, and my mother promised Wilbur that she would never get married until he came home from the war. She kept that promise although she was asked by a gentleman whom she had known, but she said she couldn't until her brother got home—and he wouldn't wait. In later years, my mother saw a picture of him in a movie-star magazine from Hollywood and he had become some kind of director. She just smiled and told me she had made the right choice when she married my dad! My Uncle Wilbur was buried with honors in Portland.

There are many more things I could tell you about those uncles from Portland—they were all part of the family who came to the ranch every summer and would stay a week or so. I only remember my Grampa Catlow—not my Grandmother Melissa, who had died before I was born. My Grampa Catlow was a full-blooded Englishman, born and bred! He had a huge family, and I have all the names and birthdates of that family in my files. He was a wonderful looking man with a mustache, and I will always remember how he poured his coffee into his saucer and drank it! He also used a cane when I knew him, so he was a little slow getting around. He would come to the ranch at least once a year and then I would have both of my grandfathers to watch and tease! Yes, I would take their canes and hide them! Then they would have to holler for me to come and find them! It was a game I never got tired of. My poor mom got a little unhappy with me, I think!

My Brothers, Sister, and Me

I was born on July 4, 1929, at the ranch. My Uncle George Vandevert delivered me. I have a picture taken that day with all the first cousins in the front yard, and it really means a lot to me. My parents named me Grace Ann, and I believe that was due to the fact that my dad had a sister Grace and my mother had two girl friends in high school named Grace. Since I was the first girl, I got the name!

My older brother, Claude, was born on November 12,

From left, standing: Betty, holding Barbara; Bill, holding Sallie Bird
On the horse: Danny, Claude, Joan, Jack, and Kathryn

1923, at the ranch. He, of course, was named for our dad, Claude Chandler. I found out in my research where the Chandler name came from—one of my Grandmother Sadie's sisters was married to a man named Chandler. I feel that is the reason for the name.

My second brother, Danny, was born August 1927 at the ranch but died in August 1929 due to tetanus from stepping on a nail. Danny was named after our Grampa Dan Catlow and his Uncle Wilbur, my mother's brother who had always been so close to her. I have pictures of Danny, and

Daniel Wilbur Vandevert

even though I didn't know him, I always wondered about that brother that I might have been so close to.

My sister, Mary Jean, was born December 24, 1934, and I thought she was my real live baby doll for Christmas that year. We have a second cousin, Mary Vandevert Curtis Hogan, who told me that my sister was named after her. The name of Jean was an old family name on my father's side of the family. We always celebrated Mary's birthday early in the evening and then celebrated Christmas.

My younger brother, Dave, was born on November 3, 1942, at the St. Charles Hospital in Bend, Oregon. Our mother died the day after Dave's birth. Several people in the family wanted to name him different names—but my dad liked the name of David. Dave's middle name, Edward, was because a wonderful nun, Sister Edwards, took care of Dave at the hospital for three months after he was born, and my dad thought that by giving Dave her name for a middle name it would do her honor. Dave told me he got to see her in later years at the hospital.

Our Home

Our home was an eleven-room log house built by my grandfather, W. P. Vandevert. He started it in 1892 right after my father, Claude, was born, and it was added to over the years and completed in 1909. There were five bedrooms upstairs and one down. There was a large living room, dining room and kitchen with pantry. The pantry was a room with cupboards, shelves and a work table where most of the bread and baked goods were put together. There was a "cooler" built into the outside wall where a few things could be kept for a day or so. We kept all of our pots and pans, dishes, silverware and extra dishes in this pantry, and it was an easy workspace to use.

Gracie, Mary Jean, Claude (1935)

We also had what we called "the milk house," right outside the pantry door. It was made of wood frame with double walls, which were filled with sawdust. It had a concrete floor and had tables and shelves for storage of all the canned goods and "store bought" goods that we had. It stayed cool in the summer time and kept the milk fresh for a few days. Then we used it for cheese and butter or for the animals. Also a small-burner stove was used in the winter when the temperature went below zero. Otherwise, everything would have frozen. Sometimes the milk would be frozen over in the pans and we would have to let it sit inside the house for a while to thaw. There was also a milk separator that was kept in the milk house in the winter-time and on the back porch off the kitchen in the summer. It separated the cream from the milk, and it had a lot of parts to it that required careful washing and sterilizing for the next batch of raw milk. It turned by a crank and really worked well, I thought! Washing it was no fun though! There was a small space in the roof of the milk-house where it was also covered with sawdust. It was a great place to play and where the cat usually had her kittens. I could play with them all I wanted to!

We also had an icehouse that was across the river from the house. It too was made with double walls and filled with sawdust. In the winter time, and this is before I remember, the men used saws and cut ice into blocks and took them up a ramp from the river to the ice-house. They would fill the interior of the house with these ice blocks and, from what I was told, it lasted them through most of the summer. I know that one of the fun parts of any get-together at the ranch in the summer was that Dad would make homemade ice cream. It was delicious! Took a while to make as it too was hand-cranked and required patience and a lot of chopped up ice and salt to keep it really cold while turning! It was always vanilla flavored and we ate every bit! It made about two gallons, I think!

Grampa W.P. Vandevert

In later years, my dad built a small one-room cabin beside the house. It was for my Grampa Vandevert, who by then was using a cane. His room had always been upstairs but it was getting more difficult for him to go up the stairs. His little one-room cabin had a bed, dresser and a small wood stove. He stayed there in the summer time. He had an Indian blanket on his bed, which had been given to him in Holbrook, Arizona, as a remembrance for his time as a Masonic leader. His routine was to come in the house for breakfast, go back to his

W. P. Vandevert

room, and then venture out to the front porch of the house and wait for someone to go get the mail. Our mail was delivered in a box out on Hwy. 97, which was one mile from the house. Our address in those days was "Upriver Route" and at one time just "The Old Homestead." That is hard to believe in this day of zip codes! Dad either drove out to get it each morning around nine or ten o'clock, or Claude or I would go to pick it up. We got the *Bend Bulletin* and the *Portland Journal*. My mother took a few magazines too. There was a lot of letter writing in those days as no one used the phones for long distance calls unless it was an emergency. My grampa would want the *Bend Bulletin* immediately—and by the time he finished with it, it would be time for lunch. He would nap in the afternoon and then go back to the front porch and sit and watch whatever was going on.

I know that one year I got my first real bicycle from my cousin, Joan, in Bend. It was a real girl's bike! Well, I learned to ride it right out beside the house and my grampa watched me try to get on, get the pedals going and then fall over many, many times. He would just watch, and if I got a little farther each time, he would laugh and let me know to keep going! I finally mastered it. He was my biggest fan and I never forgot his support! If it were wintertime, he would sit by the fireplace in the living room, and, if he could get someone to sit down, he would tell his great stories of his early days. When Grampa was in the living room during the day, he would play three games of solitaire. Even if he won a game or lost all three, he never played more than three at one sitting. He could remember trips, how many horses were taken, who the people were, and how long they were gone. One winter, after deer season, he told me to get some deer meat and he would show me how to make venison jerky like he did in the "old days." I got the meat and we cut it up in slices. We held it over the fire in the fireplace on long-handled forks until he said it was done—and then we ate it! I don't know if it was real jerky in the time we did it, but I thought it was a great deal of fun and, I think, he did too! He was a bear hunter at one time and took parties out to find the elusive lava bear. His daughter, Grace, once shot a bear when she was young, and it was written up in the *Bend Bulletin*. When Grampa died, he was buried in the Greenwood Cemetery in Bend. The Masonic Lodge conducted the service.

The Bedrooms

The bedrooms upstairs were mostly large with windows that had views of the fields and river. There was a guest room for company who might stop by. At one time, the bedroom over the kitchen was for the teacher if she needed to stay due to snowy weather. I remember one, not sure which one, who used to cut out magazine pictures and then burn the edges with a match and hang them up all over her room. I think that was an inexpensive way to decorate at that time. There were wide hallways upstairs also. They were used for various things. We had several trunks that my grandparents had brought with them years before, and they were kept either in bedrooms or the hallways. One hallway had shelves where there were many books that had been given as gifts to each other over the years. Some were from my dad's family, the Vandeverts, and some from my mother's family, the Catlows. There were also copies of old school textbooks used in school. There was also a bookshelf in the guest room that had mostly novels. I believe a lot of them came from my mother, as she had quite a collection when she married and brought them with her to the ranch. There were sets of books, novels, and some non-fiction. Some of them I read over and over again. Also, just above the wide stairway that went to the second floor, there was a small room reached only by pulling a plank, with notches, down from a small door into the room. This was called our shoe shop, where we put on new soles, new heels, and generally repaired shoes so that they would last a while longer. It was rather small to play in, but that didn't stop us from going into that little room many times.

My parents' bedroom was downstairs. It was a large, airy room with two closets and a wood stove that was used in the wintertime when the weather got cold. When I was very young, I had a bed in their room and that is where I slept until the folks fixed the upstairs room of my grandfather's for me to have for my own. I remember they wallpapered, painted and put new quilts on my bed—and I thought it was wonderful to have my own room. I filled it with books, pictures, and kept the trunks that had always been in the room there. I also had a dresser for all my girl things! I remember buying cosmetics from coupons in the magazines. You could get free samples of Tangee lipstick, Pond's cold cream, Jergen's hand lotion, and even some perfumes with names that I have forgotten. It was so much fun to get a little package in the mail with some new cosmetic to try! In the summer time, we all slept outside as much as possible on beds that were set up and just left there. We loved sleeping out—watching the stars at night. It would be very cold when we arose in the morning—but we loved it.

The Outbuildings

The outbuildings near the house were the one car garage and the chicken house. The garage was located where Dad built his future home in 1953. The garage was the workshop for almost everything. Dad had workbenches around two sides of the garage where he had a large vise and a small vise. He built shelves into the walls for all the miscellaneous tools and hardware that he used every day. There was also a grinder to sharpen instruments of all kinds. A foot pedal ran it, and you had to let water flow over it as you sharpened tools. He had every size hammer, saw, bits, and other tools that you can think of. Somehow, what he needed was usually right there when something broke down. In later years, he tore it down and, in its place, he built the home that now stands as the guest house.

The chicken house was a long, one-story building and was separated into the chicken side and the turkey side by a door in the middle. We had all the eggs we needed in those days for baking and eating. We had a small flock of chickens and turkeys, which filled our needs at the time. The only other outbuilding at that time was the proverbial outhouse! It was west of the house about one hundred feet or so and, of course, was moved every couple of years to a new location. Thank goodness for inside plumbing nowadays! I do not miss that part of the ranch life at all!

Breakfast

My earliest remembrances are of the family table in the kitchen, the fireplace in the living room, and the wonderful places you could hide in that old house. The kitchen table was where we had three good meals a day. There were no such things as TV trays. The only time you saw a tray with food was when you were too ill to come to the table and your meal was brought to you in bed! The breakfast meal was always a big meal. My mother made biscuits and cooked either bacon or ham, eggs, oatmeal (which I absolutely detested) with the usual milk, coffee or cocoa. You already know that we didn't have electricity until 1941, and our telephone, a Western Electric, was on the wall in the living room. So much for utilities!

The Telephone

The telephone was on a rural line and, I believe, there were five or six other people on it at times. What that meant was that you waited for the phone to ring and count how many "longs" and how many "shorts" to the ringing. If it rang one long and two shorts, that was for us! Our phone number was 3R12. That meant we were on the 3R rural line, and the 12 meant we answered to one long ring and two short rings. I think Uncle Bill and Aunt Dorothy's number was 3R13. Whenever we had to be gone for the day, all we had to do was ask the neighbor to answer our phone and take messages. We did the same for them. There were always great stories about how, whenever the phone rang, about six other receivers were picked up—everyone was listening on the line! I don't think we had that problem, but it did happen. It was one way of hearing all the news—just like gossiping! I do know that my mother and Aunt Dorothy called each other at least once a day, if not more, and it didn't cost extra even though there were six miles between us. Bob Orr told me that Dad gave him that old wall telephone that the family used all those years, and he gave it to me a couple of years ago. It still has the batteries in it that were used and also has an instruction book about those old telephones! It is really a priceless possession!

Washday

If it was "washday," it was an all-day affair of heating water on the stove in a copper boiler, filling the washing machine and three galvanized rinse tubs and doing about eight loads of laundry—starting with the "whites" and working toward the overalls the men wore. If it was wintertime, the clothes froze dry on the line! If it was summer, they dried in no time! The whites were whiter due to the bleaching of the sun. On that day, we would fix a pot of beans, lentils, stew or something to that effect that would cook on the back of the stove without having to worry about it. That way, we were free to work on the laundry. The old washing machine was an Easy and had a gas motor with a pipe attached to take the fumes outside. I thought the fumes smelled good! When the clothes were dry, we brought them in to the kitchen table, folded and set aside all the ironing to be done the next day.

Ironing

The ironing was usually done the day after the laundry. First, we had to sprinkle the clothes with water and roll them up to be ironed later. In those days, we only had the sad irons that heated on the wood stove. We used three at a time, alternating from the hot to the cooler ones. There were two ironing boards, one of which was a flat one that could be laid on the kitchen table and I could iron the "flat" things such as handkerchiefs, pillow cases, linens and much more. My mother used the larger board for the harder-to-iron-type clothes. It usually took us two to three hours to finish. After we put in electricity to the house, a Kohler plant ran that we cranked up. It produced DC (direct current) for the power. When we ironed with the electric power, we would plug the iron in and it just got hotter and hotter as long as you left it attached. So, to cool it down for lighter garments, we just unplugged it and it cooled to a temperature we could use! We thought it was great fun and we didn't have to have such a hot kitchen to keep those old sad irons warm. At night, the last person to turn the lights off in the house would make the Kohler plant shut down. Then, the next day, we would have to crank it up again. My dad always knew when I was reading in bed at night because the plant kept running. He would finally holler and tell me to shut my light off! Then, all was quiet, and we could all get to sleep.

Sewing

Other early day remembrances were learning to do embroidery work. My mother would wash and bleach out flour and sugar sacks, which, at that time, were made of cotton. Then she would cut them up to make dishtowel-size pieces, and I would sew a small figure in a corner. I can remember some of the little figures were of teapots and cups and saucers with faces! They were so cute! Then we would iron these and they would become gifts at Christmas times for my various aunts. I tried, in later years, to use a sewing machine but failed to do a very good job. I could do patches and fix rips and tears, but that is about all.

I believe our sewing machine was a White model, the kind that you pedaled, and, I know, my mother handled it like a professional seamstress, which she was. She made ninety per cent of our clothes, at least for Mary Jean and me and herself, and the only things that were purchased were stockings and underwear and shoes, and, I guess, coats sometimes! Some of my cousins sent us a box of used clothing once a year or so, and it was like Christmas to us! I grew up with hand-me-down clothing and I thought they were wonderful. People made do and used up everything in those days! If you couldn't use it, you passed it on!

Lunchtime

Lunchtime was usually a big meal, depending upon the time of year. When the men worked in the fields and with the cattle, they were ready for a good meal! Dinnertime was more of the same and was dependent on what was happening on the ranch. It could be a rather light supper if it was a quiet day.

All the food was prepared "from scratch" by my mother. With the exception of some canned goods such as corn, green beans, and some fruits, she made meals by planning up to a week ahead. Because we had fresh milk every day, we always had cottage cheese, butter and buttermilk. I don't ever remember buying any of those things in those days. The old butter churn, a barrel that sat in a wooden support, was filled part way with cream, and then we turned that thing until the cream turned to real butter. Then Dad would work the butter to remove all the moisture and then make it into blocks of butter for future use. The Deschutes County Historical Museum now has the churn in the Vandevert Kitchen.

Groceries

We lived eighteen miles from Bend, and we had to have supplies on hand since we couldn't just run to the neighborhood store! What I remember most about our groceries was that my mother would get on the telephone to Bend and Erickson's Market and order everything she needed. Then, the clerk would fill the order at the store, and in the latter part of the morning, here would come a big truck bringing our groceries in several boxes. We had this service since the truck was on its way to the Shevlin-Hixon Camp just east of LaPine, and they kindly dropped off our order to us! Otherwise, we drove to Bend, possibly twice a month, and we shopped at Erickson's Market and filled our car to overflowing for the trip home.

Baking, Canning, and Preserving

My mother did all the baking, and I believe there was something in the oven every day! She would put together a batch of bread in the morning and make six or eight loaves. That would do us for a couple of days, depending on how many were there. She baked pies—my dad's favorite was lemon meringue—cakes, cookies, and bread pudding. She also made puddings on top of the stove. My dad had a real "sweet tooth" and liked something sweet after every meal. She provided that even if it were only some honey or jam for a biscuit after breakfast.

My mother taught me to bake and to help prepare different foods. I was the official cake-maker for birthdays and such. I even took one of my cakes, Devil's Food, to the Deschutes County Fair one year and won first prize. Those are the things that memories are made of! I belonged to the 4-H club while in school in LaPine and, in the summer, we got a week's trip to Suttle Lake Lodge for our group. Once I made a special cake for my dad's birthday! I decided it should be different! So, I made a white cake, but put blue coloring in the mix, made blue icing, and even made dark blue lettering for the top of the cake! When I presented it to Dad, he just said, "My, that is a really blue cake, isn't it?" I wonder how we gagged it down!

My mother also did lots of canning and preserving. We would get fruit by the bushel baskets and we would can everything possible. This included peaches, pears, apricots and lots of jams and jellies. These would last from one season to another, and we very seldom had to buy fruit at the store. She also canned a lot of beef and venison that we had prepared after killing and cleaning. This was necessary, as we had no way to really preserve meats. We did cure bacon and ham by hanging them in the upstairs to age and they were delicious meats.

We also had fresh geese and ducks in season, along with the fish that we caught right outside our back door in the

Little Deschutes! If Dad would say he wanted to have fish for dinner, he would just go out and catch them, clean them and then pan-fry them for supper. Talk about fresh fish! There is no taste like that. We caught German brown and rainbow trout mostly—sometimes a dolly varden. My Uncle Charlie once caught a twenty-four-inch dolly varden—biggest I ever knew of from the Little Deschutes! He thought that was quite a feat! We also had a lot of wild mushrooms growing across the river and we would feast on them when they were picked.

I can remember there was always enough food for anyone who might just happen to drop by. My mother could put a meal together at the drop of a hat! I know that sometimes a hobo would stop by for a meal, having walked a mile in from the railroad track that was to the east of us. She would tell him to chop some wood and then she would fix him a meal. I always thought that was so interesting! We had one person who used to stop by, and he could drink a pitcher of milk and eat all my fresh baked cookies in one sitting! But that was all okay in those days. He was a guest and we took care of him.

The Ranch Land

The ranch itself was 320 acres of forest, river and fields. It was a mile long, a half-mile across, and was actually in four different sections of property. The Little Deschutes River wandered through the property from the south to the north, heading for the Big Deschutes River just about a mile away in what is now the Crosswater Golf Course. The whole property was fenced and cross-fenced either with split rails or with barbed wire. I have a friend in Bend who remembers helping my dad and Claude with the rail fence and always reminds me of it when

I see him. At the entrance to the ranch, there was a big gate that had to open and shut each time we came through. Of course, this was to keep the cattle and horses and whatever other livestock we had from going out of the property! They did get away once in a while, but a neighbor would call us and we would go get them!

Years before I was born, there were large yellow pine trees, also known as ponderosa pine, on a lot of the property. In the early 1920s, most were cut off for the value of the timber and sold to Shevlin-Hixon Lumber Co. in Bend. However, there were a few that remained on the ranch that I remember so well. One that I enjoyed the most was on what we called the "Big Yellow Pine Tree Prairie" and was at the south end of the property across the river. My brother Claude and I used to go there to fish, taking our frying pan and equipment and frying and eating the fish we cooked. I thought that was great!

The property consisted of jackpine and lodgepole pine. The house sat right in the center of the acreage. The rest of the property were fields to be sown each early spring and reaped in the late summer. The jackpine trees across the river were the source of our wood for the three or more stoves and the fireplace in the living room. Wood was cut and trimmed at the site in the forest, and then the poles were hauled back to the house where Claude and Dad would use a buzz saw to cut it up to the lengths we needed. Then it had to be stacked in the wood shed. Every day they had to chop up several blocks of wood for our cook stove in the kitchen, and they would fill the woodbox to overflowing so my mother wouldn't have to go out and get more before they came home each day. Everybody pitched in to help carry in wood—just whoever was available at the time! Every day, someone had to bring wood in to the house whether it was winter or summer. Cooking and heating was needed every day. Claude and Dad took care of those chores along with many others, such as hauling in the water from the river for everyday use and getting water to drink from the pump on the back porch.

Weather

The weather played a big part in our life at the ranch. We got very little rain some years and that made a difference in how much of a crop we would get. We did not irrigate at the ranch. I believe they call it "dry" farming these days. In the wintertime, we would always get snow. Usually it started late October or November, and it would last until early spring. There were years where the snow piled up in drifts up to our windowsills in the old dining room. We could actually reach out the window and grab some snow! The snow was very dry, and when

Snow at the ranch in the 1920s

the wind blew, it would pile up everywhere! We had icicles that hung from the eaves of the house and kept getting longer and longer before breaking off. This could be dangerous if you weren't careful to stay out from under them. There were times when we were "snowed in" at the ranch until the snow plow came by and dug us out. We just kind of hunkered down when it was like that. We had a picket fence around the front yard, and one year they took a picture of Claude and me skiing across the top of the fence and through the gate! Dad would sometimes pull us behind the car on a sled too! That was a lot of fun!

We also skated both on the river and on the sloughs across the river. The sloughs froze the best, and we would go over there and spend a couple hours. Claude would always put my "clamp-on" skates on my boots and away we would go! The river could be skated on too, but you had to be a little more cautious due to the current of the river! Some places were safe—others were not! Dad and Mom could also skate, but I barely remember them doing so. I know Mom did as a young bride at the ranch—we have a great picture of her on the ice! When I was quite young, I managed to fall through the ice by the bridge. The folks had company in the living room, and so I decided to bring water from the river. I had a little pail with a handle, went down the steps on the riverbank to the hole in the ice that was kept open, and reached down to get the water. Well, I slipped in, and all I can remember is that I popped back up through the hole and grabbed something on the riverbank and pulled myself out. When I got back to the house, they said the top of my head was wet and knew I had gone clear under. Dad said the river was rising at the time and that buoyed me back up through that hole. Betty Daly told me

Claude and Gracie on skis, 1932

she was there that day and remembers it all. I don't know if I got spanked or not!

Dad and Claude still had chores to do even with the bad conditions. They had to feed the cattle, milk the cows twice a day, bring the wood in, keep the river open so the cattle could drink, and many other chores to keep things going during those stormy, cold times. The milking was done at the barn in the cold of the winter. Dad and Claude would have to take a lantern with them in the evening in order to see to milk. I loved going to watch all the activity but always had

Claude and Gracie

to stay out of the way! Claude and I can remember one year when I was small when the temperature went down to 46 degrees below zero. When you went outside, everything just glistened, and it was clear as a bell! There was ice on everything and you could hear the air crackle! The river would be frozen, and every so often you would hear a noise. It would be a crack in the ice, and it would run up the river! Also, some of the limbs on the jackpine trees across the river would freeze and just drop off to the ground! Mary Jean and I weren't allowed out in that weather! All you did was stick your face out the door and it would start to literally freeze! You learned, as I did, never, never, to stick your tongue out to get some frost off a nail up at the barn! I did that just once and lost a piece of my skin off the tip of my tongue. It froze to the nail head!

Dad and Claude had to bundle up tightly before venturing out, and by the time they got done with the chores, they were very cold! Only their eyes showed through all the wrappings around their faces! The very cold weather meant that the stoves were going almost full time. The stove in my folks' bedroom was started up during those times. Otherwise, they would breathe icy breath by morning! I just remember staying under the covers until I absolutely had to get up! Then I would run to the dining room where there was a small closet near the stove, and we could get dressed there! In fact, we kept most of our clothes there in the wintertime just because it was used as a dressing room both morning and night. Claude had a room upstairs with no heat, and he remembers ice on his blankets when he awoke some mornings! That was no fun! If he happened to have a window slightly open during a storm, he would end up with snow on his bed! I just know that we dressed very warmly and stayed in the house. There was no school sometimes—we may have lost two or three days of school, which was made up later. When the weather got really cold, the teacher would come and stay at the ranch with us until the weather broke. She just became part of the family, and we would hold class in front of the fireplace!

Holidays

In November, we had Thanksgiving dinner at the ranch and everyone came who lived nearby—Uncle Bill and family, Uncle Doc, Aunt Mittye, Aunt Maude and family, and whoever else happened by. We had a table in the dining room that had about five or six leaves, so we could seat everyone, except the children, at the main table. My mother baked the turkey, made the potatoes and gravy and stuffing, and always made my Uncle Bill a small pan of parsnips, which he loved. The women who came usually brought some of the extras. The table would be loaded, and there were usually seventeen or eighteen people who would sit down to eat. When my grandpa was living there, he sat at one end of the table and my dad and mom at the other. When my cousins and I were real young, we had to sit in the kitchen to eat—but as we grew up, we got to go with the grownups! My mother would use her best china and silver and her goblets that she had since she was married. They were in a china closet in a corner of the kitchen and were used just for those special occasions. Uncle Doc would sometimes get a call while we ate, and he would have to run back to Bend on an emergency trip but sometimes would come back later. My mother always tried to see that he got a good meal!

Christmas Day was just like Thanksgiving Day—the same people came. However, on Christmas Eve, we celebrated Mary Jean's birthday first with dinner and a cake. Aunt Dorothy and Uncle Bill would usually be there and stay all night. So would Aunt Maude and whoever else wanted to. After we had Mary's cake, we went into the living room where we had the tree, which had been up for a few days, and we exchanged gifts. The gifts came from relatives near and far, and Claude, Mary and I always had a wonderful time. We received clothes, a lot of games, puzzles, books, dolls, handkerchiefs, and many other things too numerous to mention. Then, on Christmas morning, Santa Claus would come and leave things for us in our stockings. Even Aunt Maude had a stocking, and one year she got a potato and a turkey head in her sock! I think Santa was having fun with her! After dinner, the men would play cards in the living room, and the women would visit until time for everyone to go home. I believe Barbara and I managed to get to stay with each other somehow! Depended on the weather! If it was hard to drive in the snow, I think she had to go home since we didn't know when we could take her home.

It was funny how I learned about the Easter bunny, Santa Claus, and all the rest! One Friday night, just before Easter Sunday, I decided that the bunny just might come by and leave something for me earlier than Sunday! So, I put a basket on the phonograph in the living room and waited! The next morning, Saturday, I anxiously looked to see my goodies! Well, there in my basket were three great big turkey eggs! They were brown and speckled! I didn't know quite what to think. I went to the breakfast table and Dad asked me if the bunny had left anything. I told him I thought it was odd but that there were turkey eggs in the basket! He chuckled and didn't say much more. Later in the day, while in the pantry, I noted that some of the turkey eggs were missing from the windowsill where they were kept. Slowly the light dawned! When I questioned Dad, he just smiled! So, even though the Easter bunny still came, and so did Santa, I had a deep suspicion that there was more to this than met the eye! I believed very deeply, and only after some time to think about it did I relent! Well, to me there will always be a Santa Claus, as he is in our hearts, I do believe!

Summers

The summer time was wonderful! There was usually sunny weather in the mornings, but sometimes in the afternoon we would see great big thunderclouds pile up and we would hope

L-R: Barbara, Gracie, Sallie Bird, and Mary Jean

for rain. Most of the time the clouds went away or went to the east or west of us, and we had to wait until the next time and hope we would get the rain. When it did rain, we also got the thunder and lightning and it was noisy! We once saw lightning strike two trees up by the rock pile at the entrance to the ranch! It damaged them so badly that they had to be cut down, in later years, and used for firewood. They were ponderosa pine and we didn't like to lose them.

When I think of summer, I think of swimming in the river right outside our back door! We would wait until about 11:00 A.M., and by then the water had warmed up. We would put on our suits and go swim until noon, when we were called in for lunch. What was so great was that we had a diving board and a little foot bridge right at our back door so that we could run down to the river and out onto the bridge and jump in. In those days, we had to wait a full hour before we could go back in! They said we could get a bad cramp if we didn't wait after eating. Then, in we would go again, and stay until late afternoon when Mom would call us in! We would come out looking like prunes, all shriveled up, and exhausted, and go back and get dressed and do it all over again the next day! We lived in that river every chance we got! I don't remember learning to swim—I just did! I know that our folks would be out there to keep an eye on us until we got old enough to have some responsibility! I think Claude took over watching me and then I did the same for Mary Jean! Anyone who came to swim was told to only go where it was safe and, mostly, they did. We even went in at night, and the water was so warm due to the air being so cold! We loved it! There is nothing like clear, fresh, running, river water to swim in! We all got brown as berries—and, sometimes, a real sunburn! I was lucky and usually just turned brown!

Cattle

On the ranch, we mainly raised whiteface cattle, Herefords. If I remember correctly, we would have about eighty or ninety head at one time. In the spring of the year, Claude and Dad would do the branding of the newly born calves. I got to watch the branding but thought it was cruel, even though very necessary. The brand was brought from Arizona by my grandfather and was called "The Hashknife." Then, the men took the cattle to Spring River to be left for the summer to graze. Dad would check on them once or twice a week and take blocks of salt to them. That property, where they grazed, is just west of Sun River in the foothills. Dad kept the cattle there until Camp Abbott started up in 1942, and I found out from my brother Claude that Dad used it again after the war and until he sold the cattle and retired.

He also owned the Reece place, which was on the way up to Paulina Lake, and I had thought it was used also for the cattle, but Claude said no. I think I remember once that Dad and Uncle Bill cut hay on that place but I may be mistaken. Because of the forested area and the Paulina Creek, the deer came down in the evening in droves. We counted as many as one hundred at times. They were so beautiful to watch. When Camp Abbott was built, we summered the cattle at Sparks Lake near Mt. Bachelor. Claude stayed with them that summer and had a tent that was home to him. We would go to visit him and take fresh supplies. It was such a beautiful setting. Mt. Bachelor was in the background. Claude had to be careful of his food there. He had to hang the meat in a tree so animals wouldn't eat it!

Haying

Before we took the cattle to range in the spring, Dad and Claude would plant the two rye fields. That meant a whole lot of work getting the soil ready to plant. Depending on what the ground was like, we would run the plow to cut the soil up. Then, we would disk it, harrow it, plant the seed, cover it up, and wait and pray for rain. Usually, we would get enough rain to grow the crop. Sometimes we would get a hailstorm that would almost wipe the crop out by bending the stalks that weren't mature yet. If we had a bad season, Dad would buy hay to get us through. We also cut the grass in the meadows along the river, which could be very thick and very good to put in with the rye for feed. I always watched out for the occasional garter snake that Dad would toss up into the wagon with the hay—hated that! Also, even worse, were the nests of yellow jackets which we would find and they would bother the horses too! We got away from them quickly!

My dad and mother worked together to sow the rye fields. They were a good team and they did this every spring. I know my dad would get a team of horses together, named Pearl and

The River and the Ranch

Ruby (!), and then fill the wagon with the seed that came in gunnysacks. They planted both rye and vetch. He had a big tub that he would put the grain in, and he would sit on the back of the wagon and throw the grain from side to side over the plowed field. My mother would drive the team of horses and, until I went to school, I went along. I was wrapped up warmly with coat, mitten, hat, and blankets so that I wouldn't get cold, and sat down amongst the sacks of grain and kept warm. Those early spring mornings could be very cold indeed! We would travel up and down those rows until the planting was done. I'm not sure how many days it took, but I am thinking the better part of two weeks.

The crop would be ready in the latter part of July, if I remember correctly. Dad would have all the equipment needed ready and waiting to do the job. First, he took the mower pulled by the team of horses and cut the rye. Then, Claude would come along with the rake, also pulled by horses, and get the rye into shocks along rows that were far enough apart to bring the hay wagon along side. Claude would drive the horses up to each shock of hay and Dad would pitch it into the wagon. Claude would pile it on to the slings that would later take the hay into the barn. It would take about an hour to get one load of hay. Then, back to the barn, where Claude would unhitch the horses and take them around to the back of the barn and hitch them to the pull-up ropes. Dad would attach ropes to the slings of hay in the wagon, and then Claude would have the team pull the load up and into the barn. Dad would judge where to dump the hay and pull the trip-cord. Claude would then come back to the starting point and do the same thing again, as there were always two sling loads of hay with each load.

After both were emptied into the barn, Claude would bring the horses back around to the wagon in the front of the barn and re-hitch the team. Dad, in the meantime, pulled the slings back out of the barn in the rafters down to the wagon and placed them in readiness for the next outing for a hayload! We kept a count of each load brought in, and at the end of the day, we would see how many—sometimes up to eight loads and sometimes only five or six. It depended on where in the fields the hay was and how much. The whole job of getting the crop in took about two to three weeks. If I were doing my part of this job, I would take ice cold water to the men from our back porch pump at the house. It was the best water I have ever tasted! Also, we made homemade root beer in the summer, and I would bring that to them in the afternoon for a refreshing drink. When I was old enough and reliable (!), I drove the horses sometimes, and that gave Claude a bit of a break!

In later years, in fact 1942, Claude was working in the Forest Service and was away from the ranch that summer. Dad and I put the crop up, and I think we did a pretty good job! It was hot and tiring, but Dad was good to me and we always rested a while after lunch, got a second wind, and then went out and got three or four more loads that day! You knew you had done a day's work by the time dinner came around! That was the first time that Claude had been gone for any length of time and I missed him with a passion! I thought I had lost my best friend, and I guess I had! That was such a surprise to me that I would miss that brother who teased me and who I managed to give a bad time to so many times—but, I guess, there was a bond there that came out when we were apart.

Claude and I were together so much as children, living on the ranch and growing up there with chores we each had to do. He was always the one who helped me with anything that I thought was too much for me. He put my skates on, kept my skis waxed, watched me when we went swimming, taught me to ride a horse, showed me how to milk a cow (even if I really only did that a few times), and he was just a great big brother. He played ball with me and even let me bat once in a while. We built dams in the spring when the snow melted and ran towards the river. He would make paddle wheels, and I could spend hours watching them turn in the little streams of water. We tied flies together that we used to go fishing in the river. I tagged around with him all the time

Claude, Mary Jean, and Gracie

49

whether he liked it or not! I always thought he could do such interesting things, even though I look back now and think that it was probably just part of the chores and responsibilities he had on that ranch. When he left home to go to work, I found that I not only loved him very much but respected him too for all those years of work. It goes on to this day of being together and talking about that time of our lives, both the good and the bad, and being very humble about the parents we had and how they raised us.

After the haying was done for the day, or even any workday with the horses, the men had to take the horses into the barn and remove all the harness gear that was used. It was hung up on the wall of the barn and then the horses were turned out to pasture until the next morning when it all started again. I know that after working in the fields all day my dad and Claude would each grab a bar of soap and head for the swimming hole to bathe! The river was warm at that time of day and it was a great place to take a bath!

When all the haying was finished, we brought the cattle back from the range. Then, sometime in the fall of the year, my dad would decide which cattle were to be sold. I cannot remember all the details except that one year we took them to a railroad-loading place close to the Paulina Ranch, and they were loaded and taken to Portland, I believe. A few years ago, a friend showed me where those stockyards were in Portland and I tried to imagine Dad being there. He would stay overnight at the nicest hotel in Portland. I think it was the Benson Hotel. I guess that happened each year, and it was well deserved, as that was our paycheck for most of the year in one lump sum! I know that Dad also sold some of the beef in Bend to local meat markets. In later years, I believe Dad had a truck that he used to haul some of the cattle to Bend or wherever he sold them. I just am not sure! I also have a vague feeling that there were trucks that came to the ranch and picked some of the cattle up to take to market! Anyway, the main thing is that they were sold!

During the summer, we had many people visiting the ranch. Some came for a few days and others for a week or two. There were always lots of people at that wonderful old house. I grew up knowing all my aunts and uncles and cousins. They came and went all the time, and my mother loved having them. Also we lived within a few miles of the Shevlin-Hixon Lumber Camp which was to the east of Highway 97. The people who lived there often came to the ranch to go swimming or picnic. My folks designated a few acres of grassy land on the Little Deschutes at the north end of the property and allowed families to come to fish, swim or picnic there. Some years, in the wintertime, they flooded a portion of the area and had an ice skating rink where people came from Bend and LaPine to skate. In the summer, they put in a wood floor platform and it was used as a dance pavilion. Again, people came from near and far to dance by lantern and moonlight. I have friends in Bend who still remember that era. I can barely remember it—only that I saw people dancing and I thought it was wonderful!

My Dad's Family—The Vandeverts

Just to understand why there were so many people coming and going, you must know that my dad's family had eight children. Only the youngest, Arthur, was born on the ranch. The others were born in Texas, Arizona, New York and Powell Butte, Oregon. My dad was born just a couple of months before my grandfather came to the ranch to start building and

L-R: Bush, George, Mittye, Claude, Bill, and Clint

homesteading. This was 1892. Dad was born at Powell Butte at the home of his grandfather, Joshua Jackson Vandevert. My grandfather (W. P.) and grandmother (Sadie) had come from New York to get settled on the ranch on the Little Deschutes River. As soon as Claude, my dad, was born on January 6, 1892, they waited until Sadie was up to it and then moved to the ranch. There had been a small building on the ranch when they got there and they used it to live in until the house started to go up by the river. It was built a little at a time until it was completed with eleven rooms. I believe I once figured that it had about 4000 square feet on both floors.

This family who came there were really remarkable people! Somehow, they eked out a living using various methods to gain income. My grandmother kept travelers overnight and would charge them room and board. These were people traveling from Prineville or Shaniko heading south towards California. There was no town of Bend at that time, only a couple of homes of early-day settlers. There were some early-day people in Prineville—and that is where my great-grandfather,

Joshua Jackson Vandevert, lived. Mostly, these were men. Grandmother Sadie also had the mail concession at the house—she didn't like doing it—got rid of it once—and then got it back later. But someone had to do it! My grandfather was a well-rounded person who could make a dollar one way or another. He did all types of work, such as making snow sleds, hunting trips for bear, surveying roads in the mountains for the government, raising cattle, and trapping in the river for fur skins. In later years, when my mother came to the ranch, she took over a lot of the duties that Sadie had done. She tells in one letter how seven or eight people came by and stayed overnight and that she cooked for them and got them all bedded down and was very proud that she could handle this chore that went with being in charge.

There was a great deal of trading and swapping in those days also. Some of the furniture I grew up with came from trading with other families. I know that the neighbors would trade meat when they butchered, and then we would trade back when we did our butchering. It helped in those days because there was no refrigeration. Meat could only be kept so long unless canned.

Grandmother Sadie taught the children until they went

Sadie Vincentheller Vandevert

into Bend for schooling. She had been a teacher, and it surely shows up in her children. They all became very useful citizens in later years. Most of them went from high school on to college. Three of the boys became doctors, the three girls became teachers (one with additional Bible studies), and the other two boys, Claude and Bill, stayed in the ranching business.

Mittye

Mittye was the first child born to W. P. and Sadie. She was born on August 17, 1883, in Fort Worth, Texas. She actually stayed with the John Cox family, her aunt and uncle, in New York, when the rest of the family left there in 1891. She was a wonderful lady who lived in the South part of her life and then went to California and finally back to Bend where she lived her remaining years. She had a master's degree in religious education from Columbia University in New York City. She never married. She was a "giver" of herself to many people. While in California, she did secretarial work for the Methodist Church and, as I remember her the most, she came to the ranch to care for us after my mother died in 1942. I first remember her in Bend in a little home where she cared for her Aunt Mittye, who, at that time, was an invalid. Her church was her first love and her family loved her very much. She died February 5, 1975, in Bend.

William T.

The second child was William T. (Bill). The family then lived in Ft. Griffen, Texas. Born on December 16, 1884, he was my Uncle Bill. He and my dad were the ones who decided that ranching was for them, and that is where Uncle Bill stayed until his health failed. He lived at Paulina Prairie in a two-story home on a ranch and raised cattle too. Claude has told me that Uncle Bill and Dad were equal partners in the business until Uncle Bill and Aunt Dorothy left Paulina and moved to Tumalo in 1935. In the early days of that partnership, they ranged the cattle at Davis Lake, some distance from the two ranches. The ranch at Paulina Prairie was only about six miles from our ranch, so we were together a great deal of the time. He had a huge barn and other outbuildings on his place. I remember that his brother-in-law, John Brazil, built a play-house for Barbara, my cousin, and we used to play there every time I visited her. I also remember the big old frogs that were under the house! We played with them too, even though I don't think we were supposed to!

My dad and Uncle Bill traded work with each other. When one was needed, the other came to help. Uncle Bill's ranch also had some race horses at one time. His property had an irrigation ditch so that he could water his crops. Barbara and I played in it—getting in lots of trouble for doing so as the water was very swift! My mother and Aunt Dorothy shared the washing machine at the ranch, as the water at Paulina was evidently not sufficient. Also, the Dalys, our neighbors to the north, where Crosswater Golf Course is now, shared the washer. I remember them well—and Betty still lives in Bend. Aunt Dorothy and Uncle Bill and Barbara would come down periodically to do their laundry, and we would fire up the washing machine and go through the laundry. It lasted most of the day. My mother and my Aunt Dorothy were very close sisters-in-law and loved each other dearly. Actually, they were second cousins before they married the two Vandevert boys, so they hit it off in many phases of ranch life, each helping the other.

Uncle Bill and Aunt Dorothy moved from Tumalo to just east of Pilot Butte on a small acreage that was less work for them. By that time, Aunt Dorothy was working at St. Charles Hospital, and that is where she worked until she finally retired. The last few years of their lives they lived on West Thirteenth Street in Bend in a little white house on the corner. By then, Uncle Bill was getting older and that is where he finally passed away February 28, 1969. Aunt Dorothy managed to keep up with her wonderful sewing and also did a project that is now in the Bend Historical Museum. She made doll dresses of inaugural dresses of all the First Ladies of our land and used materials almost to the exact likeness that the dresses were made of. She hunted long and hard for just the right doll to dress and just the right piece of material and wasn't satisfied until it was done right. She eventually gave them to the Historical Museum where they make such a great exhibit. They are well worth seeing. Also, she found dolls that needed new clothes and made new outfits for them, and then she gave them to the church to be sold. I have one of them. Aunt Dorothy died in Bend on September 24, 1984.

Barbara, My Cousin

I could go on and on about the relationship I had with my Uncle Bill and Aunt Dorothy. They were such an integral part of my life—it was like having a second mother and dad. Their daughter, Barbara, and I played together more like sisters from as far back as I can remember. We are only six months apart in age, and we had a very special relationship. I can remember knowing that they would be coming to the ranch and I would go outside on the front porch with my grampa and watch for their car. You could see the dust rise from the road a ways out

L-R: Gracie and Barbara

from the ranch and, since there were so few cars in those days, I would watch breathlessly for it to be Uncle Bill's car. If it wasn't, I just waited again. When they finally came, Barbara and I had a life of our own to play and explore and only come in for lunch when we got called. We went swimming, hiking up the river, up to the barn, caught crawdads in the river, fished, and just had a wonderful time.

We almost managed to drown one time while our mothers were doing the washing! We were playing in a shallow part of the river with a sandy bottom, and I happened to push it a little by going too far down the river where it got deeper and deeper! I started to yell–so did Barbara–as I was caught in the current. I knew better! Barbara started after me–and she got caught in the same current. By then, my folks heard us yelling–thank goodness–and my dad came running–taking his shoes off as he ran–and he jumped in after us. I was going down for the third time, so he pushed Barbara towards a willow close to where she was–and he dove after me. He pulled me up, coughing and swallowing half the Little Deschutes River! He took me to the bank of the river, helped me get a grip on the edge, and then got Barbara from the willow! Well– as you can guess–my mom said later that she didn't know whether to spank us or hug us! I don't remember getting spanked–but we two girls were in a heap of trouble for some time! When it came time for them to go home, we would both beg and plead to get to stay with each other—either Barbara would stay with me or I would go home with her. We nagged our folks until they couldn't handle it any more and gave in. When they moved to Tumalo, about twenty-eight miles away, we got to ride in back of Uncle Bill's pickup truck—all the way! We loved it! Tales of Barbara's and my escapades never end!

Maude

The next child born to W. P. and Sadie was Maude. She was born February 22, 1886, in Fort Worth, Texas. As far back as I can remember, she was part of our family too. She had three children. The first was Bill, who was also the first child born to this large family and became the first cousin of this generation. Then Kathryn and Betty came along. Their father was Chester Catlow, who was a musician and played the organ music in the theaters in Portland before the "talking movies" came along. I also believe that he had a pharmacist's license, and taught music. I only met him once in later years as he had moved to the Caribbean Islands and lived out his days there teaching music to the natives, and that is where he died December 22, 1974.

Aunt Maude was a teacher of the highest caliber. To this day, I have friends still living in Bend who tell me how much they loved her and how much she influenced their lives. One such person is one of my oldest and dearest friends from that era, Virginia Russell Ferguson. She and I were best friends from the time we met at LaPine. She loved her teacher, Mrs. Catlow, and, in the future, she too became a teacher. I get to see her every few years, and we love to talk about those wonderful days! I stayed with her many times in Shevlin, and she came to my ranch to stay with me. I took her back to the ranch a year ago, and we had a great time remembering "back when!"

When I first knew Aunt Maude, she was teaching at the Shevlin Camp east of the ranch. I visited the school there when I was very small and then would stay with her in her little camp cabin. Well, I never stayed very long—I would get terribly homesick and she would have to drive me home! Not even getting to sleep in her bunkbeds was enough to keep me there! And she was so good to me about it—just packed me up and took me home! She would come to the ranch about once a week, if I remember right, and she would do her dry-cleaning out on the porch with some kind of solvent that really smelled bad! Then she would hang her clothes up to get dry, and they would be all ready to wear again. She used to clean and can chicken. She knew that I liked chicken necks, so one time she canned a whole jar just for me!

The Shevlin Camp was a unique place. The Shevlin-Hixon Lumber Company employed all the families that lived there. The families all lived in the same type of homes that could be lifted and put on a railroad car to be moved to a new location. Friends of mine, still in Bend, lived there and can tell great stories of those days living in the camp cabins. The grocery store, the church and the school were all railroad cars fixed up to service the needs of the people. I thought it was so much fun to go to visit the camp and see all these homes amongst the huge ponderosa pine trees. They would cut timber in the area and then move to another area. The moves probably happened every seven or eight years.

After Shevlin School, she taught in LaPine in the first and second grade—all in one room. I visited there too, and she was so nice to those little kids. She would play the piano for them, and I never heard her raise her voice. But she also kept the discipline! I can't imagine anyone talking back to her! I was never a student of hers as I didn't go to school in LaPine until my third grade, but I got to stay with her in her little home in LaPine. It was bigger than the Shevlin Camp home—and she had it filled with pictures that I loved to look at. She was living in Bend at the time of her death on September 30, 1945. She had a stroke, I believe, and I got to see her before she passed on. I remember how badly I felt at her funeral, as it was only the second funeral I had been to. The first was to my grampa's—but he was very old and I didn't feel quite as bad. My family didn't let me go to my mother's funeral—so I think I related my mother's funeral to Aunt Maude's. I missed Aunt Maude—she was always good to me! She would bring dresses from Portland for Barbara and me to wear and we thought that was great!

Bill

Bill, their first born, worked for the Forest Service in his early years. He married Cleora Vaughn, and they had a daughter first, Rena Rae, and a son, William Jr., and they live in Bellingham. Bill passed away a number of years ago. He was such a wonderful older cousin to me and to my family. My dad loved him very much, as did my mother. It was always fun with him around. I wrote to him during WWII and he wrote back to me! I loved that. Aunt Maude's family came to the ranch often and, again, were part of my childhood. It was like having an extended family because we knew they would always come there whenever possible.

Betty

Betty was a nurse and trained in Portland. My mother would write letters to her to keep her from getting lonesome for the family back in Central Oregon. She was also a talented seamstress and helped Barbara make her wedding dress and all that went with it. She married and had a little girl named Julie, whom I haven't seen since she was a little girl. I believe she lives in California. Betty died at an early age, and it was a tragic loss to such a wonderful cousin.

Kathryn

Kathryn too was so special! I can remember how she would take Sallie Bird (another cousin-daughter of Uncle Bush and Aunt Martha), Barbara and me up to Elk Lake for three days at a time to camp out! That was quite a handful for one lady! She was so much fun! In later years, when I was in high school, in Bend, and had to stay overnight to go to Job's Daughters, she would have me come to her apartment and we would have grand talks about everything and anything. One thing I remember was that during World War II when everything was rationed that she would mend her silk hose if she got a snag in them and was able to make them last a lot longer than I ever did in later years!

Kathryn worked for the Forest Service in Bend, met Don Erickson, married him, and are now retired and live in McMinnville, Oregon. My sister, Mary Jean, was their flower girl and they married in the Episcopal Church in Bend. They have two daughters, Bonnie and Jeanie. Don loved to fish at the ranch when they visited. I am so lucky to get to visit with them at least once or twice a year, as we all meet in Bend for reunions of the LaPine-Shevlin group. All the people who come to that picnic have a story to tell her of their wonderful teacher, her mother, Mrs. Catlow.

Clint (Uncle Doc)

The next child born to Grandfather W. P. and Grandmother
Sadie was John Clinton, in Holbrook, Arizona, on January 13,
1887. He died in Bend on March 14, 1967. He was my Uncle
Doc. I never called him anything else. Friends called him Clint
and J. C. He was a doctor in Bend for over fifty years. He and
his brother, George, were together as doctors for a few years, in
Bend, but George moved to the Oakland area and set up practice in the early 1930s. I don't remember George in Bend,
even though he delivered me and signed my birth certificate!
Uncle Doc and Aunt Harriet lived in what was once a hospital right on the river near the Pine Tavern in Bend. It was a
lovely home that I delighted in visiting. It had so many rooms
to explore! And they had real bathrooms! I thought that was
wonderful, and I would go in and just turn the water on in the
basin and let it run! At the ranch, we had to heat water on the
stove, drag a large oblong tub into the kitchen and then take
our baths in front of the stove. It took a long time out of an
evening for all the family to bathe.

Their children were Jack and Joan, and they were two wonderful cousins who always treated the younger cousins like
they were grown-ups! I have never forgotten that! Jack had a
pool table, and his friends would come in after school and
play. I could sit in a window seat and watch them, and I
thought that was great fun. Jack would bring his friends to the
ranch lots of times, and the one I remember the most was Bert
Hagen. Bert was a special friend, and I am in touch with him
to this day. Jack would bring a gun to the ranch to shoot, and
Dad would tell him where it was okay and he would be careful
not to scare the livestock. He and Bert were both great bird
hunters and used to go to Eastern Oregon to hunt and bring

back ducks and geese. Bert and his wife still live in Bend, and they keep me posted as to what is going on in my old hometown.

Uncle Doc (known as Clint to most) was the medical doctor who would make house calls. You don't find them these days. He would get a call while just sitting down to dinner and have to leave everyone and go to the hospital or to some other emergency. When he would come to the ranch for dinner on Thanksgiving or Christmas, we always knew if the phone rang, it would be for Uncle Doc. My mother would always hope that he at least got a good meal before he had to leave for Bend. My mother loved Uncle Doc and Aunt Harriet, and they were always welcome back at the ranch.

My mother sometimes went to their home in Bend to do the laundry in the wintertime or if our washer wasn't working. I was allowed to explore the big house with all those rooms! In the very back was a library where you could curl up with a book, and there was a huge living room with a fireplace at one end that always seemed to have a fire going. Out from the living room, library and bedrooms, was a huge wrap-around deck that was so roomy with lots of wonderful chairs and lounges to sit on—also a porch swing! Down from that porch was a beautiful big grassy lawn with a weeping willow tree on one side and ponderosa trees, and it went to a high bank with a path down to the river. Since those days, the home has been torn down and there is a parking lot in its place. Jack would feed the ducks and geese that congregated on the Big Deschutes River, and he was known far and wide for calling them to eat every day!

Jack

Jack also was an avid hunter, fisherman and athlete. In later years, he had a sawmill in Eastern Oregon, and he died very unexpectedly of spinal meningitis at a very young age. It was a shock to everyone. I have never forgotten him and what a loss it was when he died. He and his wife Joyce had one daughter, Jill, who was very tiny at birth—almost didn't live—only weighed a couple of pounds. This was before incubators. But she hung on with the help of great nurses and my Uncle Doc, her grandfather, and she grew to be a beautiful woman with children of her own. She and her husband, Steve Ziegman, now live in Arizona and I try to keep in touch! Mike Brown, his stepson, still lives in Bend.

Joan

Joan was my wonderful cousin who always showed me a good time when I went to her house in Bend. She had her own room, and I remember a desk where she did pen and ink drawings. One of her favorite drawings was of Betty Boop, a cartoon character of the day, and was popular again in 1998! Joan would take me to movies, fix me lunches, and just generally let me hang out with her. She also gave me all of her Big Little Books, which were so popular in those days, along with a whole set of Nancy Drew mystery books. I would take them back to the ranch and arrange them on my shelves! Then, she would bring her girl friends to the ranch to visit and go swimming. There would be a whole car full empty out and lots of yelling and hollering at the swimming hole! Joan was a princess in the Bend Water Pageant that was held every Fourth of July in Bend on Mirror Pond. The Deschutes River slows down into big bends right in the heart of the city, and this is where they would build an arch and all types of floats would come through—the first being a huge swan with the queen and then three or four small swans with the princesses. Joan still meets with those friends from that time of her life. She was a very popular girl in Bend and had many life-long friends. When Joan was in nurses training in Portland, my mother wrote to her to keep her up to date with what was happening back at the ranch. Joan still tells me of those letters to this day, as they meant so much to her.

In later years, she married Bob Orr, and they have Nancy, whose children are Janet and Elizabeth. Next born was Keith and his children are Matthew and Gregory. Then, Lori Jo, last but not least, came along! Now, Bob has retired from the Union Pacific and is active with the Masonic Lodge. He and Joan live in McMinnville and they are very happy there!

George

Uncle George was the next son, born on December 3, 1888, in Holbrook, Arizona, and died in November 1972. He went to Columbia in 1923 for a year of postgraduate work. He learned about making baby formula (Carnation) from canned milk. He brought the idea back to Bend and had the people in the Shevlin-Hixon Camp give it to their babies. This was due to the raw milk being delivered to the camps. It was sometimes spoiled, and the children actually died. After bringing this formula, the infant mortality rate lessened. He was married to Olgamarie Paulsen, who died in 1947. She had been a nurse during World War I. He and Uncle Doc were partners in Bend for a few years, and then Uncle George and Aunt Marie moved to the Oakland/Piedmont area of California in 1930 where he had two offices. One office was in downtown Oakland and the other was down on the waterfront where he would go two or three nights a week to take care of the black people. They loved him. I think he did this without pay if the people were poor.

Vincent, Allen, and George Jr.

I really didn't know Uncle George and his sons until 1947 when their mother died. They came to the ranch that summer, and I got to see them for the first time. Claude, I believe, remembered when they were in Bend, but I was too small. The next year, 1948, Barbara lived with them and went to college at Berkeley, and I got to visit them for a week! They had a wonderful big home in Piedmont, which had thirty rooms! Each bedroom had a bathroom! There was an intercom system in the house, and the first morning I was there, I heard someone call my name! I couldn't figure it out and finally saw the box on the wall! It was their housekeeper telling me it was time for breakfast! We had a wonderful time that week and that is the only time I have ever been to the Bay area. Since then, we keep in touch—Vincent lives in Anderson, California, Allen lives here in Gig Harbor after retiring from Weyerhaeuser Company out on the Key Peninsula, and George (Bud) died in 1996 in California.

Kathryn Grace

Kathryn Grace Vandevert was born in New York in 1890. The family had moved there from Arizona, and Grandma Sadie's sister and husband lived nearby. He was a pharmacist in New York City. She grew up on the ranch and loved it dearly. We have her diaries, letters, and other things that helped us figure out what kind of a wonderful girl she was. She and my dad were very close. Grace died in November 1918 of the terrible flu epidemic that hit the whole United States. Thousands of people died. She was only ill for a few days and just couldn't throw off the after effects of that terrible flu. There were not antibiotics, as we know them, at that time. She was only twenty-eight years old, and it hit the family very hard. Uncle Bush, her younger brother, wrote a poem about her after the death. She is buried on the ranch, and I think all of my sons know where that is, just south of the house on the riverbank. How I wish I had known her—she sounded like such a great person! I have a small blue and white trunk and a ring of hers. I take great care of both!

Claude (My Dad)

Next born was my dad, Claude. I could go on for pages about him. He was born January 6, 1892, in Powell Butte, Oregon, just between Redmond and Prineville—a short way past Powell Butte on the way to Prineville on a road to the right called Stillman Road—up Stillman about a quarter of a mile to the sharp turn. Stop and look up on the hillside and you will see a huge old barn that was built by my great-grandfather and his sons in about the 1880s. They came there from Cottage Grove where his wife, Grace Clark, had died. He and his two sons are buried in Prineville next to each other. They are Charles and Walter Vandevert. Their other brother, Dick, was buried in Yoncalla, Oregon. Dad died on December 5, 1975.

Since Dad was born in the wintertime, the family waited until early spring to move to the ranch and start to build a home. Dad lived on the ranch all of his life except during World War I and a time when he worked as an electrician in Portland and down on the Columbia River near the Hood River, on the Washington side. When he was away, he was so lonesome, and I have those letters that tell how he misses the family and to "please write"—he loved their letters. He finally left that job, which my brother Claude tells me would have been a very influential job in his later years. All the men he worked with liked him, and the bosses gave him better jobs, as they could see his potential. But, as you know, he loved the ranch too much and headed back there as soon as he could. I believe part of his earnings were sent home and each of the boys helped each other out with the education at the colleges where they studied to be physicians. I'm sure that my Grandmother Sadie made the money stretch in every way possible, and she was adamant about education, having been a teacher in her younger years and then teaching her own children.

Arthur (Uncle Bush)

The last child born at the ranch was Arthur (Bushie) on November 27, 1894, and died June 16, 1972, in Sellersburg, Indiana. The nickname of Bushie came because he had such a head of hair! Have been told he didn't have a first name until he was four years old, at which time he named himself! He too studied to be a doctor. I believe all of them went to Willamette University for their education. He married Martha Shadburne Whitcomb and, because his mother had come from Kentucky originally, she wanted one of her sons to go back to that area to live. So, that is where my Uncle Bush and Aunt Martha lived for as long as I can remember. They had a home in Sellersburg, Indiana, and Uncle Bush practiced there and in Louisville, Kentucky, just across the river.

Sallie Bird and Cynthia
They had two daughters, Sallie Bird, who is my age, and Cynthia, who is Mary Jean's age. They would come out to the

ranch every summer for about a month. One time they came by bus into Bend (they may have ridden the train from The Dallas) and we picked them up there and took them to the ranch! The car was full! They stayed in the north bedroom upstairs and, of course, the girls slept with Mary and me. We had a wonderful time with the girls there! We could get into more trouble than you can believe! But, somehow, we lived through it. Just think, there was the Little Deschutes River right at the back porch, bridges to cross, barns to play in, animals to ride and just be around, and all sorts of things to keep little kids busy getting into trouble. We were given limits and we always exceeded them! Barbara would be with us as much as possible and we were called "The Three Cousins"—my poor sister was younger, and I know we probably pushed her aside as being too little to join us! Kids can be so cruel! But she and Cynthia

were the same age and, I guess, since I can't remember all that, they got along okay! I know I was always unhappy when it was time for them to go back to Sellersburg, Indiana, where they lived.

One time, when I was about eight years old, my dad took me to The Dallas to pick Sallie Bird up at the train and bring her back to the ranch. Her folks came a few weeks later. That was my first, I think, overnight trip with my dad. We stayed at

L-R: *Mary Jean, Barbara, Sallie Bird, and Gracie*

the Dallas Hotel, ate dinner, and then went to a movie! That was such a treat. The movie was *Abe Lincoln in Illinois*—and I have never forgotten that time. When I got back to the hotel, I was already lonesome for the family at the ranch, so I wrote a letter to them! I still have it —it was in the things from the ranch, and it is funny! Well, the next morning, Dad and I picked up Sallie Bird and her escort nicknamed Shog, I think, as he was Uncle Bush's chauffeur, at the train and started back to the ranch. That was a great trip for me, even though I didn't like riding in the back seat!

It wasn't long before her folks came, about July 1, I think, and they stayed until the end of that month. Uncle Bush always had to come back to the ranch! He and Aunt Martha loved it and once told my folks that when they retired they would like to come back there. Of course, that didn't happen, but not because they changed their mind. World War II changed everybody's life from there on. Anyway, Uncle Bush was having trouble with his eyes in later years and that hindered his work, but he still had an office and could diagnose just as before. He died June 16, 1972.

Aunt Martha was born February 24, 1899, and died in 1995. She was a priceless lady with a Southern heritage! My mother loved her so much. They were almost the same age— just months apart. They wrote to each other all the time, and my mother would read those letters—full of things about Sallie Bird and Cynthia. And, I'm sure, my mother wrote about the ranch life and us back to her! If e-mail had been in that era, they would have been on it every day, I'll bet!

Aunt Martha could knit and sew, and every year she would send Barbara, Mary Jean and me something to wear. I especially remember a skating skirt—mine was blue corduroy on

L-R: Jeanie, Martha, Dorothy, and Mittye

the outside and red lined inside and, when you wore it, it was beautiful! In her later years, she used to call each of the first cousins and get brought up to date with what was going on in our lives. She finally had to give this up due to weakness. Her daughter Cynthia went to see her every day at the nursing home in Sellersburg where she died.

When my husband and I came back from Philadelphia in 1954, we stayed at their home for two days before coming on back to Bend. They were so good to us—they had a bad lightning storm just before we arrived—and so they had no electricity and we went out to dinner. I thought that was such a treat! It was also very humid and hot, and I was seven months pregnant with John, so they gave us their air-conditioned room. Now that was a sacrifice!

I have named all of Dad's family, and I know I will think of many more things about each and every one, but the main thing I shall never forget is how close they all were. They had a bond to the ranch and to each other that never went away. They lived to be together, both as youngsters and later, as adults with families. They always gravitated back to the ranch. I guess that is the way I feel, even today, that it is a pull on my heart that will never be replaced. But life goes on, and I only look back to keep the memories of all this and feel very lucky to have been born and raised there.

Everyday Life in the 1930s and 1940s

For the everyday life at the ranch, it was different every day! For one thing, we had no TV to watch. We had a little battery-operated radio that, if I remember correctly, ran for one thousand hours, and then we had to purchase another battery. That meant that we didn't just turn it on any old time. My mother listened to some daytime plays that ran for fifteen minutes each! They were like our present-day "soaps," but let me be clear, they were very bland material! They were just stories of daily lives of people—and, of course, left you hanging at the end so you would turn them on again the next day.

They advertised soaps, cereals, shampoos, and any number of items, just like the TV does today. You just listened to it! In the evening, there were great radio shows on with people like George Burns and Gracie Allen, Jack Benny, Bob Hope, and hundreds more, and also shows that had a whole story in one sitting—maybe a half-hour long or one-hour. There were contests like *Major Bowes Amateur Hour* where people liked to sing, tap dance, play an instrument, or do very funny things too. Some of the people who went on to be successful in the movies, theater and so forth, got a start there. We would all try to guess who would win the contest, and the audience would clap for the ones they liked at the end. By the way, Major Bowes lived in Tacoma at one time and he is the one who helped develop Fircrest—he named the streets, etc.—and you will see his name there. Claude also reminded me that Major Bowes was convicted after the war of spying for Germany!

Once in a while, when we went to Bend for shopping, our folks would let us go to the movies in the afternoon. That was usually about two hours. I think it cost a dime to get in, and then we would buy cracker jacks or popcorn. There were no ads then. There would a "coming attractions" film to let us know what new films would be shown next. Then, there would be the news of the day. It would show a portion of a speech by President Roosevelt or show what was happening in the rest of the world. It would have funny and sad things in a short ten minutes or so. Then there would be the cartoon, usually a Walt Disney one, and it was always a lot of fun! Then the main feature would start. I actually see some of those old movies on TV to this day! Talk about taking you back to your childhood! One thing, they were almost all family-oriented films. You could take your kids with you anytime. Nowadays, it is so different! When we would come out of the theater, it would be about time to go back to the ranch. Once in a great while, as a family, we would go at night to a movie that both Dad and Mom wanted to see! That too was a treat.

When I was quite small, my mother would take me to the J.C. Penney store in Bend just before Christmas. We would go down in the basement and that is where all the toys were! And, I'll never forget, they always let me ride a little red tricycle around the basement, even though it was for sale. I just loved that and couldn't wait until I was big enough to have a real bike! I had some growing to do!

Back at the ranch, we had a victrola, radio, and a player piano (which is sitting in my living room right now). My son

Tom has the victrola. People would come there in the evening and bring other instruments to play, and we would have a wonderful time. Some would dance too. Other times, we would go to a neighbor's house, such as the Dalys, and do the same thing. I was quite small in those days and can't remember the details but I know that went on long before I was born. Music was a big part of our lives from the time I can first remember. I know that I had to stand up and sing sometimes for relatives that came, and the song I remember most was *Springtime in the Rockies*. In later years, my sister Mary and I would sing all the latest song hits of the day. I taught her to sing *God Bless America* for one thing—and we taught our little brother Dave to sing *Old Buttermilk Sky*!

When Uncle Bush and family were there in the summer, we always had a barbecue on the Fourth of July just across the bridge amongst the jackpine trees. People came from all over, especially from Bend. All the relatives came who were in the area, and a lot of Mom and Dad's friends came from Bend such as the Magills, the Coyners, the Cashmans, and many whose names escape me now. This was all in the 1930s and I was quite small. I just knew it was my birthday and didn't realize until later that it was also Independence Day! I have some pictures from that time, and it is fun to try to figure out who everyone is! Dad did the barbecue and all the women helped with setting it up and furnishing the food. We hung a huge American flag, and it will be at the High Desert Museum if they want it. We always had a flagpole out in our front yard where Dad always flew the flag on any holiday! Oh, yes, I almost forgot that Uncle Bush always gave me a silver dollar on my birthday! I held on to them for a long time!

When my mom was still alive, we went to dances at LaPine

in the wintertime. They were held, I think, once a month at the little Pioneer Hall, and we had live music—banjo, drum, piano, and maybe more—but they played waltzes, one steps, two steps, and a lot of square dancing too. That is where I learned to dance, as Dad's men friends would help us "little" kids with square dancing and we thought it was wonderful! It would last until about 1:30 in the morning, and then we would have to drive back to the ranch where Dad would light a fire in the dining room so that we could get warm enough to go to bed and not freeze! It would be very cold—lots of times down to zero—so a fire was wonderful!

After my mother died in 1942, I finally got my dad to take me back to those dances in LaPine! He and I would leave from the ranch about 9:45, drive up there, stay until about 1:00 A.M., and then drive home. He had a lot of his old friends still there, and I was old enough by then to have boys ask me to dance! In fact, I had one boyfriend who lived in Chemult, about forty miles from LaPine to the south. He would drive to the dance, and we would spend the night dancing together. Then, when it was time to go home, he would go home in his car back to Chemult, and I would go home with Dad. I went with him before I graduated from high school and think we had about two nighttime dates! He came to the ranch and, I think, liked to talk to my dad as much as seeing me!

My dad and uncles and cousins also took short trips in the summer time to the lakes. We would make a day of it—with a picnic lunch—and go to any number of lakes nearby. One of my favorites, which I only saw one time, and that was Waldo Lake. I believe it is one of the largest lakes in the Cascade Range, at least in that area. I thought it was beautiful. Someday I'll have to go back and see it! I would guess there is a paved road to it now! One summer, my dad and Uncle Bush and Uncle Bill took all us kids to Cultus Lake, and we stayed for a couple of nights! That was a real treat! We didn't have sleeping bags in those days—we just rolled up a bunch of bedding and pillows and away we went! Uncle Bill could cook anything over an open fire and we had plenty to eat. That is what my dad's family did regularly in earlier days—go up to the lakes and pick berries to bring home to can. Cultus Lake was absolutely beautiful! It was so clear that you could see to the bottom! It was all sand and had a bit of a tide that would wash up on the shore. We could only swim in the shallow parts, as it was really cold a few feet down! It was so beautiful up in those mountains! There were only dirt roads to get up there so there may have been only a couple other families there at the same time. In later years, with paved roads, it had people there all the time! I scarcely recognized the place a few years back!

People always asked me if I didn't get lonesome at the ranch without any close neighbors! I always thought that was so funny! I didn't know what the word meant. There were

Gracie and Mary Jean on Dolly
(when they were younger)

things going on there all the time. I don't really remember a dull day! Claude had a wonderful horse that we called Pepper, and he was used for the cattle roundups. He was a first cousin to the racehorse, Man O' War, and in later years was stolen from the ranch. We advertised in five states to no avail. That was a real loss, especially to Claude.

I had a horse, Nellie, that had a white nose and was a strawberry roan. Dad got her for me when I was about nine, I think. Before that, I rode a Shetland pony called Dolly, and she was a lot of fun. There are several pictures of her in my albums. She was ornery too and would try to scrape me off if she could! And she did a couple of times!

When I was about eight years old, I took my fishing pole and walked across the big bridge behind the garage. I had a steel rod approximately four feet long that I used all the time. I used whatever bait I could find and that was mostly grasshoppers. This day, I dropped my line in the water, watched it flow under a willow and soon felt a tug. I gave a yank and then let out a yell!! I pulled in a beautiful 16 ½ inch German brown trout that weighed

Gracie

over two pounds. I yelled for my dad to come and see, and he came and watched me pull it in. Then, my mother took pictures of me and the fish and, later that day, my grampa called the local *Bend Bulletin* to tell them about it. They put it in a local column the next day, and I have never forgotten that fun time.

I also got to ride a little red Hereford bull that Dad bought one year. It was a gentle animal, and Dad would put me on it while it was eating hay and let me ride around the barn yard on its back! We also had a "bummer" lamb or two every year. Those were the lambs that the mothers wouldn't accept as their own, and to keep them alive, we would bring them into the house in a box and feed them milk from a bottle with a nipple. I don't ever remember losing any of them, and as soon as they were old enough, we put them out with the rest of the sheep. We had one old pet from as long back as I can remember that we called Bo Peep! What else! She had a long tail, which was unusual, because tails were usually chopped off right after they were born! She was just a pet that hung around wherever she wanted!

We had the usual chickens and turkeys too. They produced eggs that we used every day. Someone gathered the eggs and fed the chickens and turkeys, and I just remember that I hated the turkey gobbler. He chased me. Barbara and I both got in trouble for going near the chicken house, simply because the old gobbler would always chase us. Barbara remembers the only spanking she ever got from my mother was because the two of us had sneaked out to the chicken house and the gobbler ended up chasing us. My mother had warned us time and again not to go there! Well, we each got spanked but can't remember if that stopped us!

There were the usual dogs and cats. The two dogs that were always there, I remember, were Tippy and Nick. They were both just plain, good, old dogs, and we took good care of them. They would always bark if anyone came in the front gate. Cats were either barn cats or house cats. All that meant was that the cats at the house ate there and stayed outside, and the barn cats stayed at the barn and Dad fed them there! Cats were only allowed in the house to play with for a while and then out they went! I know they had plenty of holes to get in upstairs if they wanted to! I also had a "pet" bullfrog that, I thought, came back every year just to see me! I made him a home in a hole near the river, lined it with cloth, and, for some reason, that darned frog only stayed a few days and was gone!

One year, in the spring, I learned a lesson that I have never forgotten. Across the river from the house were a lot of willows close together. I walked over there and noticed that there would be a bird's nest in each of the willows—sometimes two. I got to thinking that it would be real nice for all those baby birds to be able to have friends close by. I went from willow to willow gathering up the nests and bringing them all back to one huge willow tree. I distributed them all around and in and out of the branches and thought I had done a really great thing. Now all the birds would have playmates.

Well, when I got home about an hour later, Dad said that he couldn't understand why the birds were making such a fuss over in the pasture. I told him I had just been there and that they were all okay. He asked me what else I had done and I told him of putting all the nests in one willow. He just took my hand and away we went across the footbridge and over to the big willow. He didn't have to say a word as I could soon see what I had done. Here were all the mother birds trying to find their own little babies and to no avail. Some of the birds were dying and I learned a very hard lesson that day about leaving birds and animals alone in their own places.

Dad took me on a couple of trips when I was young. One was to the ocean, and I think it was Depot Bay. We got there after dark and stayed in a big old hotel close to the water. I didn't see the ocean until the next morning and I was fascinated. He took me to the Sea Lion Caves and I thought it smelled terrible! At the gift shop, I remember buying my mother three pictures. They were scenes of the ocean with seaweed around the edges and in nice old frames. I have them now hanging in my bathroom and they give me a lot of good memories.

Another trip, about 1941 or so, and I believe Mary Jean went too, was over to Brownsville in the valley to visit with the Kummler family. They had an orchard and Dad and I picked fruit to bring back to the ranch to can. I think that is the trip that we hit something up on the Pass and had to do something to the car—have just forgotten what! While in Brownsville, we went through the woolen mill that was there. Well, we got a guided tour through. We started where the raw wool was cleaned and separated and on farther to where it was made into yarn and thread, and finally into blankets. Well, again, I have never smelled anything so bad! They used some kind of acid to clean the wool and it just made you ill! I tried to hold my nose, but that didn't work. When we finally got to the end of the whole thing where the blankets were made, the smell had let up. Dad let me pick out any blanket I wanted, so I got a saddle blanket for my horse Nellie. All I remember is that it was gray and it worked just fine! I rode bareback a lot, so it didn't get too much use!

All of my sons have been to the Lava River Caves that are just a few miles from the ranch. I started going there before they put a real trail through it with wire so you could guide yourself. My dad and any family who happened to be at the ranch would climb Lava Butte just for fun. Afterwards, we would go through the Lava River Caves. One time, Dad, Claude and I went down into the entrance to the cave without a lantern, as we just wanted to check it out. We had been through the cave many times and that is when you rented a lantern from Mr. Nedrow at the entrance or else you would get lost. Well, this time, we just walked back as far as we could see and found a big rock where we just sat down. We could see the entrance—just a big, lighted hole—and here came a group of people. We just watched them coming down, and there was one fellow who was the leader who acted like he wasn't afraid of anything and was bragging about going first into this black hole. Dad decided to have some fun. He took two matches, lit them up, and held them side by side to look like eyes and then gave out a terrible yell! This fellow stopped short, looked, couldn't see anything, and started down again. Dad did it once more, and, I think, this fellow was the first man out of the cave! He ran out and all his people followed! We got quite a laugh out of it. When we came out of the cave, there they were telling about the animals that must be down there! I always thought that was great fun! No one got hurt and I don't think that fellow bragged again very soon!

We had visitors several times a week. It was sometimes people we knew or just someone looking for directions. One summer, when I was about ten, a great big touring car came into the ranch. A man got out and asked my dad if he could fish in the river. Dad said, "Okay, Gracie will show you where the fishing holes are down in the bend of the river." So, I waited for him to get his fishing tackle out of the trunk of his car, and when I saw what he had, I just about fainted! He brought out a tackle box that was huge—that had layers of drawers in it with every kind of fly, hook, bait, leader, line and gadgets that you could think of. He asked what to fish with— so I picked out what looked like a Royal Coachman fly and told him that would do. Claude and I tied a few different kinds of flies, but I had never seen the amount of fishing equipment that I saw in that tackle box.

We walked down to the bend of the river and he talked to me all the time. He asked my name, and all that, and then he told me that he lived in Hollywood and that he made movies. I guess I asked him what movie he had been in. He told me he had been Captain January in a movie with Shirley Temple and his name was Guy Kibbee. I had seen the movie, so I was quite impressed! He did catch a trout, and when we walked back to his car and put his things away, he thanked me for taking him fishing. Then he reached in his pocket and gave me a quarter! Well, that was a lot of money in those days! I then told him that I also had a brother and a sister—so he gave me two more quarters! I look back now and wonder where I got the nerve to do that! I just didn't think it was fair to get that money for something fun and not have Claude and Mary Jean get in on it! Guy Kibbee made several movies, and they were fun to see having met him that time.

Another time, a large car came to the ranch, but he was expected. His name was Irving S. Cobb, and he was a writer of short stories and a book or two. My grampa had taken him bear hunting years ago and he came back to visit with him. They sat out on the front porch. My mother and I had made tollhouse cookies and homemade ice cream just for his visit. We brought some out to him and he looked at it and said, "I'm not supposed to eat anything sweet, I have diabetes, but just give it to me—it looks too good to pass up!" And he ate it all! A little while later, my nanny goat came up by his beautiful big car and jumped up on the running board, up onto the hood, and up to the roof, and stood there looking at us! I was mortified to think she might scratch his car! But he just shook with laughter and said he would never forget his visit to W. P. that trip! Irving Cobb was a wonderful old man and he wrote about his bear hunting with Grampa in earlier years. Somewhere, I have that story!

One summer, in late August, I think, a plane ran out of gas and landed in our rye field. It was just a single engine plane, I think. The pilot and another person came to our door and asked to call Redmond to get some fuel brought to them. So, that meant they stayed for a while! Well, curiosity got to Claude and me, and we wanted to see the inside of the plane! Do you know those people wouldn't let us in! I thought that was very bad manners when they landed in our field and needed our help! Claude may have gotten in later, but I know I didn't! I have never forgotten that! It was just a small thing to ask of them and they turned us down! Oh, well, it was still exciting having the plane land there!

We also had yearly visits from the Irish sheepherders! They came every spring on their way south for grazing and would stop off at the ranch overnight. They camped in the upper field, and Dad would let me go with him to visit them in the evening. One time, we got to eat with them. Sometimes, they would leave the male sheep, bucks, with us to keep until they came back in the fall. Dad would let them graze in our upper field. When the bands of sheep came by out by the road, just east of the ranch, you could see the dust rising long before they got there! There would be hundreds of sheep to a band. I'm not sure how far south they took them, but think it was a good sixty to seventy-five miles from our place. We had a few heads of sheep that we kept at the ranch. We would shear them once a year and sell the wool. I think it probably brought in a hundred dollars or so at that time. I was allowed to pick up the scraps of wool that were left over, put them in a gunnysack, and then I could either sell that for money or get a subscription to a magazine for the value of the wool. I know I got magazines, as that was the best deal, I thought. That was important to have a regular delivery of magazines to keep up with the world! I know we got *Colliers, Readers Digest, National Geographic, Saturday Evening Post,* and other women's magazines that I can't remember at this time. I got one called *Wee Wisdom*—and I loved getting some mail just for me!

In the fall of the year, we would get our annual visit from the Indians. They would come in the morning by car and have horses and supplies with them. There probably were about thirty adults, because I think they pitched about four or five tents in the upper pasture. They were there to go hunting for deer, and they would stay about two weeks, I think. This was a fascinating time for me! The whole families came and brought their children and even little babies, called papooses. The men would go hunting and bring back the deer meat and hides. The women would prepare the hides for tanning and making moccasins, gloves, clothing and many other things.

One year, Dad gave them his hide, and they made my mother some beaded moccasins and a pair of gloves for Dad. They may have done that every year, but I just remember one particular year. The beading was done so beautifully. However, I did not like the smell of that smoky material in the house! Mom's moccasins were really smelly, I thought! We provided the Indians with fresh milk each day—maybe other things. The Indian children would come down in the evening, come in the house and just sort of sit and listen. It was a little hard to get them to talk, if I remember right. But they would bring a papoose with them, and I got to hold it in its cradle. It was a wonderful experience! My grampa was very good to the Indians and they loved him. The older men of the tribe would come to visit him in the living room and talk about old days. Grampa could speak a lot of their language. I heard a little of it but mostly I stayed out of the way. When the men came in from their hunt, they built a "sweat house" made of willows bent over to form a dome-shaped little room. Then, they would heat rocks in a fire outside the house until very hot, and they would bring buckets of water from the river into the little house and dump the rocks into the water. This would cause a steam like a sauna bath, and they would sit in there for some time. Then, when they were done, they would run out of the little house, stark, staring naked (!!) and go jump into the river! I suppose they did this to close the pores. They were very healthy people, so I guess this did them a lot of good besides giving them a good bath! I thought it was a great way to bathe!

I wasn't allowed up at the camp when all this was going on—I had been warned by my folks to stay away from the camp until later in the evening! Later, I knew why! I got to go "skinny dipping" all the time, but not when anyone else was around! Most of the time, we wore bathing suits! That was just in case we couldn't run back to the house if someone drove in! The Indians would leave just as they had arrived—very quickly and quietly. They always left things just as they found them and then they were gone. The next year would come and they would be back. I always thought this was so special. I have tried to find out more about where they came from. After all is said and done, we think that they were some of the Warm Springs tribe. I have tried to find out to no avail.

In those early days, Claude started school at the little schoolhouse across the field. It was a one-room school with a cloakroom to hang coats. There were some shelves in the main room, and that is where supplies and library books were kept. Claude went clear through his freshman year there and had one particularly great teacher, Mrs. Caldwell! She was a sweet lady and we knew all her family. They came to the ranch often and we went to visit them when they lived at Brown's Creek. Claude, I believe, thinks that she gave him a very good start in life from her teaching.

Sometimes, there were only two or three at school! The Dalys would be there, and I have some pictures of some of the others who I can't really remember too well, in some cases. Claude would go down to the school about an hour before school started, and he would build a fire in the stove. Then he would pump some water in a bucket and also clean the floors. He was the official janitor and, I think, he got paid about $5.00 a month—maybe a little more! He really earned it!

I started there in my first grade and had a teacher, whom I did not like! She'd get on my case, and I really did not like my first grade of school at all! I would start pleading with my mom

The Little Schoolhouse

to let me stay home, but she was smart enough to make me go to school! And, I guess I learned something—I got to go to the second grade the next year! Then, Claude and I had the most wonderful teacher, Ford Hunnell. It was his first teaching job at our little schoolhouse. He drove from Bend every day. He was not only a good teacher, but he would play ball with us at recess and always had a smile. He was a genuinely nice man, and at the end of the school year, he took us on a picnic over to Big River and treated us all to hot dogs and other picnic things. I have never forgotten him. He went on from that little, one-room school to become a principal in schools in Deschutes County. I started to like schooling that year.

The next year, Claude and I had to go to LaPine to school. Dad had to drive us there every morning and then come back in the afternoon to pick us up. That amounted to fifty-six miles a day for those two trips. It took time from Dad's work, but it was a sacrifice that my family made to see that we got our education. The school was from the first grade clear through your senior year of high school. It was two stories high, including a large basement and gym. It is gone now—lasted until about 1992 when a big snowstorm dumped a lot of snow on the roof and it caved in! It hadn't been used as a school for a long time.

Claude was, by then, a sophomore, and the little school couldn't handle all the classes he needed in high school. I was in the third grade in a room with both the third and fourth grade. Our teacher was Miss Olin, and she lived with her father, I believe, just a block or so from the school. She was a very pretty redhead and, I suppose, she married in later years. After the fourth grade, I went to a class with both the fifth and sixth grade in one room. I had a wonderful teacher, Mrs. Howard. She was an older lady and always smiled a lot! We had a lot of fun in those classes, and because there were only fifteen or so kids in a class, we learned a lot! Claude was across the hall in the high-school room with freshmen, sophomores, juniors and se-niors—all in one room! I think his teacher was Mrs. Rose—I may be wrong! Anyway, when he graduated from LaPine High in 1940, he was only sixteen years old. He had started to school when five years old and took the fourth and fifth grades together back in the little schoolhouse on the ranch!

Since Claude was only sixteen, he decided to take a post-graduate course at Bend High School, so I started my seventh grade at Allen School, which is where the Safeway Store is on Third Street in Bend. This was the year 1941-1942. It burned down in later years. My sister, Mary Jean, started at Reid School, which is now the Bend Historical Museum Building. Claude drove us every day and dropped me off at Allen School, and then picked me up after school and back to the ranch we went. By the way, Claude also drove us to LaPine the last year or so and that was fun! We drove an old Model T Ford, I think, and the radiator was really a mess—lots of holes—so we would fill it with cornmeal and that would fill those holes a little, but finally the radiator would boil over and blow back into the windshield! What a mess! But, Claude would fix it some way and away we would go to school! We sometimes got to drive the better car—or, sometimes Dad would drive us to LaPine. I look back now and think of the sacrifice that my mother and dad made of going to LaPine every day.

While I was at Allen School, I worked in the principal's office every day for an hour to help the secretary. I filed all the excuses that the mothers wrote to the school as to why their kids didn't make it the previous day or so. I thought it was a lot of fun and I read some pretty funny excuses. One asked that they excuse her son "because his big toe hurt." I thought that was hysterical! I don't think we would have gotten away with that! I had three or four teachers in that school, whereas I had only one previously. One of my favorites was a friend of our family—Cornelius Aloyisus Patrick Mahoney! They called him "Connie"—and he and the gym teacher, Dorothy Slusher, went together and finally married in later years. I saw him in 1992 in Bend and we had a good chat! His mother once taught at the little schoolhouse on the ranch, which I didn't know. When I started looking up the history of the ranch, I found some of those facts as to who taught there. I still have friends who went to that old Allen school! Also, Dad or Claude was driving us to Bend every day to school! This amounted to seventy-two miles a day just to get that education!

By the 1942–1943 era, I was in the eighth grade at the Bend High School. It was, and still is, located just two blocks from the downtown Bend. It was right across from the Deschutes County Library too, and as I am writing this, there is a new library being built just a block from that one I went to so many times! This was such a big school compared to where I had gone before. For each class we went to a different room. It was two stories high, plus a basement. It had a huge gymnasium right next door where we had all of our gym classes. It had a swimming pool that we got to use some of the time.

As eighth graders, we were "low men on the totem pole." Everyone took advantage of us, but we survived to become freshmen. From my sophomore year on, as soon as I was fifteen years old, I got a student permit to drive a car to school. While Camp Abbott was there, I got to drive a jeep out on our field, and all I remember was how hard it was to steer. There was no power steering in those days. You just pulled on the wheel and hoped for the best.

Since we lived eighteen miles from Bend, it was cheaper for the school district to buy a car for us to use. In other words, a school bus would have had to come to the ranch, eighteen miles, each morning, just to pick my sister and me up, take us into Bend, and then bring us home after school. That would have been 72 miles a day for a big school bus, and it wouldn't have been good on a business basis. I got my special license and thought it was great fun to drive. I had a really nice 1940, four-door, Chevrolet sedan with a stick shift, of course. I knew how to drive with the old type shift in the floor of car, but this had the stick on the wheel, which was neat. My driver's license restricted me to just drive directly to the high school and back. On the back of the license it said, "Proceed east to Hwy 97, proceed to Bend city limits, proceed to Franklin Ave., proceed to Bond St., turn left, and drive to school and park. Return by the same route." I never stayed within these restrictions—I was all over the place. Those were the World War II years, so our speed limit was 35 miles per hour! Ha! Sometimes, I stayed in that limit!

I also had a "C" stamp for gas, which meant I could have all I needed. I was considered a school bus! Other people that just drove to work or around town got only "A" stamps which, I think, was either three or five gallons of gas a week and was used for personal use. A "B" stamp gave you more, I think, and it was for business use, but I have forgotten. I think Dad was allowed a "B" stamp for having a ranch which, I suppose, was considered a business. It certainly was a business and I re-member that he bought a fifty-gallon barrel of gas that was delivered to the ranch so that he didn't have to drive to Bend for a fill-up. The whole idea was to use less of everything in those days! So, here I was, driving to school at the age of fifteen, and I never knew until I went back to my twentieth class reunion that I was the envy of all the boys in school! Most of them had no cars and those that did only had an "A" stamp, which didn't take you very far!

I was allowed to stay in Bend once in a while, overnight, with a girl friend, usually because of a football game. I then took all the kids home afterwards in my car and I guess they still remember that to this day! I just thought it was great fun! Dad and I had a deal about it all—if I decided to come home after the game, I had to be back by 11:30 P.M., or he would start to worry! If I wasn't home by midnight, I knew he would be terribly worried, so I always tried to make it before 11:30 and I don't ever remember him yelling at me about being late! He gave me a lot of room in those days! I graduated from Bend High in May 1947, and had made many friends, some of whom I see to this day. We were all very close and we took care of each other!

World War II started in December 1941. The Japanese had struck Pearl Harbor and it was a terrible shock to the whole world. Life, at the ranch, changed a great deal after that time. In 1941, I believe, that was the last summer that Uncle Bush and Aunt Martha came out until after the war in 1947. All travel was restricted because of the war effort, and we went on a lot of rationing.

The worst thing that happened to our family at the ranch was that we lost our mother in November of 1942. She was 42 years old and was to have a baby in January 1943. She hadn't felt well for a couple of days and asked me to stay home and clean her bedroom on a Monday, November 2, which I did.

Pearl Catlow Vandevert

That night, about 11:30 P.M., she went into a coma and Dad called Uncle Doc to come right out.

He arrived in about twenty-five minutes. I stayed with Mom while Dad cranked up the Kohler electric plant for lights. She kept asking for me and didn't know me when I told her I was right there. I was thirteen years old and had never really been around someone that ill. I rubbed her arms for her, as she said she felt numb. Then, Uncle Doc got there and took one look at her and called Bend for an ambulance. He had me go out to the dining room with him and he asked me to stay at the stove and heat some water to boiling, put a hypodermic needle in it, and let it boil for a few minutes. I did that and he went back to Mom. The next thing I knew, the ambulance was there, and I peeked out in time to see her wheeled out of her bedroom and be put in the ambulance and taken away. That was the last time I ever saw her.

I knew she would be okay when she got to the hospital. I went to school the next morning and my Aunt Mittye came back to the ranch with Dad to help out. When I came home that night, Dad said he would be going back to see Mom and she was pretty sick. I understood that and went to bed. The next morning, Dad took Mary and me to school. About one o'clock in the afternoon, when I was going from study hall to the library upstairs at school, I got a real funny feeling like something was wrong. I didn't know what to think. I knew that my mother would be fine, as she was in the hospital and that is where people got better. My brother Claude, who had been away in Corvallis at Oregon State College, met me after school with Mary. He also had my Uncle Charlie, who was my mother's brother from Portland, in the car. I was so excited to see Uncle Charlie, and I remember asking him if he knew our mom was ill and in the hospital. He didn't turn around and seemed so quiet. Well, then Claude was the one to reach across the back seat and put his arm around me and said to me, "You are a big girl now, aren't you?" Of course, I said yes. Then he told me our mother had died that day at about 1:00 P.M., and I always wondered later if that was why I had such a strange feeling at school that day at just about that time.

I just plain didn't believe it, but something told me I had to act sad—so that is just what I did! I tried to cry! I put on quite an act and really did feel badly for Claude and Uncle Charlie, as I felt they really thought they were correct. They took me over to Uncle Doc's house and that is where I found my dad sitting in the living room. His face looked so sad and I told him I would take care of him.

My Mother Pearl
(in her wedding dress)

He told me that there was a baby who had been born on November 3, the day before Mom died, and they didn't know how long he would live because he wasn't due for a long time. He was a seven months' baby! They didn't have a lot of chance in that day. That night, I heard my dad cry for the first time and it is etched in my memory. It was so deep and sorrowful, and I began to suspect that something was terribly wrong. Why else would he cry?

The next day, Thursday, I went to school, and even on the day of the funeral, Friday. The family thought I shouldn't go to the funeral due to my age! How I wish they had let me! I needed to know that she was really gone! That Friday night some of my aunts came to the ranch and we carried on. It took a week for me to finally reconcile myself that she was really gone! I just couldn't believe it! I was thirteen years old, and I think I turned into a real nasty little girl for a while! I didn't want anyone to do anything for my dad—I wanted to do it all, as I was so sure I could take my mother's place. I didn't want anyone else to iron his clothes or serve him dinner! Can you believe what a little character I was? Well, I was bad and even worse at times. In later years, I apologized to my Aunt Mittye for being such a brat, but she said she didn't remember it that way. Well, I knew I had been bad and, at least, I eased my conscience a bit!

She was a wonderful person who tried so hard to take care of our family, which she did! As in everything else, time begins to heal when you are busy, but there were so many times I wished I could hug my mom and tell her how much she meant to me. You only have one mother, and I was so blessed with mine. She was a real saint and everyone who knew her loved her. Many of my old friends tell me to this day how they loved her, as did all the family. I just wish she could have known her grandkids! She and I made a pact when I was about ten years old. We decided that neither of us would ever smoke! I said that if she started smoking, I would leave home, and if I started to, she could leave home! It was just a joke, but, somehow, I never forgot it! Maybe it is what kept me from it, maybe not! I did try once and thought it was awful! All I wanted to do was brush my teeth! That was the end of that trial!

When I was in grade school in LaPine, my mother drove me to my piano teacher twice a month for lessons. Her name was Mrs. Chamberlain, and it cost 50 cents a lesson! It was quite a sacrifice in those days and I have to admit that I did not become a piano player! I just didn't take to it! Now, I look back and wonder why I didn't try harder! I envy anyone who can play a piano! This was one of my true regrets!

In later years, I was told by many people that my dad and mother were the two most in-love people they had ever known. My brother and I have talked about that and agree that only one time did we ever hear what might have been considered an argument! It had to do with Claude and me getting at each other over some darned thing and one thought he was to blame and the other thought I was to blame! It lasted all of five minutes, if that long, but it was the first time I ever heard a difference of opinion between them. I was so naive that it was a shock when, in later years, I found out that married people have arguments and fights! It sure didn't happen in our house! I have a lot of their letters before they were married and they show the love that was between those two people.

That little baby, born the day before our mom died, was still getting stronger all the time! We named him David Edward, and he stayed in the hospital until February of 1943. Then, my Aunt Mittye came to live with us and she helped take care of that little boy—a lady who had never married and hadn't been around many children, but she took over and really made a home for us! She stayed with us through the summer of 1943, and then we took Dave to Portland to stay with our cousin, Elizabeth, who had just adopted a little boy the same age. She kept Dave until the following spring. I got to go visit him once. Claude and I went over in the spring after school was out and brought him back home. By then, it was 1944. We took

David

care of him that summer, and then we took him to Bend to a friend whose husband was in the service. Her name was Connie Tyson and she had two little girls. She kept Dave that winter and Mary and I also moved in with her. That was nice, as we could be together while we went to school. The following year, Aunt Dorothy took Dave with them to Tumalo, and after that winter, about 1946, Dave was able to stay at the ranch.

He started to school down at the little schoolhouse, and

there were a few other kids there with him. To me, what is so remarkable, is how he turned out to be such a wonderful man! He had been around so many people, most of whom loved him dearly, but really didn't get to settle down in his home until he was five years old or so. I so wanted to quit school and take care of him, but Dad wouldn't have it—said education was too important. So, like in Dad's day, we made do as best we could. Dad did what was best for all of us at that time! He kept us together as some of the family offered to take each of us to help out. He felt we could manage and, somehow, with loads of help from that family of Dad's and Mom's, we did. I have never ceased to be amazed and thankful that he kept us together at that awful time in his life.

World War II

I have told you before that World War II started in December of 1941. It was a time of gas rationing, sugar rationing, cigarette shortages, tire shortages, and even clothing—shoes were scarce, and hosiery was almost impossible to get for the women who worked in offices. You heard about some going in to the Wetle's Department Store and you had to go line up to get two pair. The nylon was needed for the war effort. I helped sign people up for the sugar rationing cards, and when I was fifteen years old, I got to give my blood every six weeks or so at the blood bank. I had to have Dad sign a special paper to give permission for that.

I also had what was called a "Victory" garden that was next to the large garden that Dad put in every year just across the big bridge. It had been set up so that everyone would get interested in growing their own vegetables, and in that way more could be sent to our troops. I think a group of people from the Home Extension Agency out of Redmond came one Saturday and judged my garden! It was quite exciting! They looked at what was planted—carrots, beets, onions, turnips, spinach, and other root vegetables—and they gave me a blue ribbon for mine! That meant a lot! I really felt I was helping our soldiers!

Another thing we did in those first war years was to become "plane spotters" for the government. This meant that every time an airplane came within view of the ranch, we would go out and check which direction it was coming from, where it was headed, and what the body of the plane looked like to see if we could identify what kind it was. Then, we would call Redmond at the center of all this in Central Oregon and report what we had seen. They would have other "spotters" along the way that would continue to phone in when it was seen. I never did find out if there were any "enemy" planes that we called in! I doubt it very much, but it made us feel like we were, again, helping the war effort! We also saved tin foil that we would get from gum and other packages, roll it into a ball, and take it to Bend to drop off someplace where they collected it, again for the war effort.

In 1942, Camp Abbott was built where Sun River is now. It was an Army Engineering Camp, and, at one time, it had ten thousand soldiers there. They basically learned to build things and bridges were the most important. Claude reminded me that these engineers at Camp Abbott were the ones that re-built the bridges to allow American troops to enter Germany. This would have been in 1944 and 1945. They also learned their artillery prowess, as we could hear the guns at the ranch going off all the time. They shot the big shells from one side of the river to the lowlands across the river, right where we would normally have had our cattle! We found the trees shot up in later years! Dad had sold the cattle when the war started.

There was also the Women's Army Corp. stationed there too! They were called WACS, and I thought their uniforms were not very feminine! We could go down to Camp Abbott for special parades and so forth, so we got to see the soldiers march and to see all the barrack buildings that had been built in just a short time. There was a huge hospital unit there and Aunt Dorothy worked there until the war was over, I believe. It was one long building with wings off the main floor and just ran forever! I got to go through it once before it was torn down after the war.

We watched the Officers' Club go up with all those logs and that huge fireplace! It was quite something to see in those days! We heard that the Colonel wouldn't give any of the soldiers working on it any leave until it was finished! It stands today as the only building left of the original buildings during those war years. It is now called "The Great Hall" and is a central part of the Sun River complex. It was recently refurbished and the lighting is much better now. It still looks wonderful! Meetings are held there, and the place is always in use for seminars and many dinner parties and other recreational activities. I believe a church service is held there too. The rest of the buildings of Camp Abbott were all torn down and taken away. Also, I almost forgot, there were Italian prisoners of war who were brought there during the war after Italy was captured. Dad always felt sorry for them as he drove by their camp, he told me. They had their camp right close to the bridge on the south end of Sun River. I know they were treated okay while there. Dad said they were and were fed well. It was probably better than being back in Italy at the time!

Dad was a civilian guard for the Army when they dismantled Camp Abbott. He sometimes worked all night and, I know, one of his jobs then was to drive around the perimeter of the camp and check to see that nothing was getting in that shouldn't. If he worked during the day, we took his lunch down to him and stayed with him for a couple hours. He had a regular uniform and hat, and we kept his uniform clean and ironed so he really looked wonderful. I think he enjoyed a lot of that time as he saw a lot of people coming and going. Some would stop and visit with him. And he got a regular paycheck. I don't know what kind of money he made, but I'm sure it was fairly good pay at that time.

While the war was on, there were also a lot of soldiers right outside the fence at the ranch. They had maneuvers, and a group would come for just a few days, practice whatever they did and leave, and another group would come. I remember that they had "tank chases"—they actually ran up and down the road between Thousand Trails area and where Sun River is now and chased each other! It was so noisy, and I had to stay clear away from the road at that time! The dust was terrible, but I suppose it was a lot worse in those hot tanks. I remember that a soldier was run over and killed out east of Pilot Butte. He had been sleeping behind a log and was unaware that the tanks were out chasing, and we all felt very bad about that. The men who were there for that training usually stayed for anywhere from a couple of weeks to several months. Then they were sent away, overseas, and they are the ones who built the bridges in the European theater of the war, especially in France and Germany. It helped win the war. Claude said that this was the 4th Corp. that came to Central Oregon, and there were 100,000 troops there at one time!

Because these groups would come and go every few days, they buried all of the foodstuffs that they had on hand, so they could order another batch for the next group of soldiers coming in! Dad found out about it and said, "Don't bury that stuff!" So, they would bring us tins of meat and cheese, and we would take it to people who needed it. They also buried food that had been fixed for meals, but never eaten, and it was cooked in huge barrels on the cook stoves. So, Dad made a deal with them to have them bring it to the ranch and dump it in our barrels across the fence. Sometimes we went out to pick up the food ourselves with our truck. We had two barrels, I think, and they would fill them with the remains of meals such as spaghetti and meatballs, stews and all kinds of food. We bought about fifty or sixty pigs and fed them that summer with that food. One time, there must have been several dozen hard boiled eggs in that food—hadn't been peeled—and we tried to keep them from the pigs, as Dad thought it might not be good for them to eat the shells! We didn't lose any, so guess we did right! Dad always said that the pigs ate better that summer than some of the folks he knew!

Some of things that I remember most about those years from 1941 until the war was over in 1945 was how lonesome those soldiers were whom we saw all the time. There was only one other Army Engineering Camp in the USA at the time, and it was on the East Coast. So, what did the Army do but send the East Coast fellows out to Oregon and our fellows back to the East! It was the first time I had ever been around black men. They were very nice, and one day two or three were hanging across our fence up at the barn looking down at the river, so Dad asked them if they would like to come in! There were signs posted all over the perimeter of our ranch that said "Off Limits to all Military Personnel," and that meant no soldiers could come in to camp. Dad said it was okay as long as he gave permission for them to visit. Of course, they did, and then they wanted to ride the horses! Dad said they were just "work" horses, not for riding, but they didn't care! They asked if they could please ride them in the pasture. So Dad made a halter of rope for them, and they got on those old work horses and rode them bareback all over the upper rye field—and had a ball! They just loved it! We thought it was all so funny! Some of the other soldiers came down and fished off of our big bridge. Dad made them poles from the willows and furnished them with hooks and bait and they fished for hours! Dad knew how to treat them, as he had once been a soldier in WWI back on the East Coast in New Jersey and had been very lonesome!

Dad kept me pretty restricted on the ranch when all of this was going on. I could ride my horse Nellie around the fields but wasn't allowed to go out on the roads. One day, I rode down by the schoolhouse, and there was a soldier hanging across the fence. He asked me what my horse's name was and I told him. I asked him what his name was and he said, "Hoiman!" I said, "Hoiman?" And he said, "Yeah, yeah, Hoiman!" Well, finally I figured it out—it was Herman! He was from Brooklyn, New York, and I had never heard that accent before! My dad laughed a lot when I told him about "Hoiman!"

Another soldier by the name of Bill Moyes came to the ranch and visited lots of time with the family. He had come from the Southwest, I think, and was around for about two months. When he left, he wanted me to write to him, which

I did. He wrote long letters to me and once sent me a shell bracelet from the South Pacific somewhere. He stopped writing at some time, and I never knew what happened to him. I always wondered if he made it through the war. He was very likable and loved to come and have dinner with us. I just hope he got home okay after the war.

This was all happening when I was between fourteen and sixteen years old! It was quite an experience at that time, and I have never forgotten those lonesome soldiers. In the fall, after we got the hay in, they would come down and pick up the hay we missed and stuff it in their mattress to make it more comfortable, as they all slept out in those days and it got very cold at night! I would help them pick up the hay and, I think, they enjoyed talking to civilians like us!

I remember when the Japanese surrendered. I was on the Oregon Coast with the Crosby family. We were staying at Twin Rocks, just to the north of Tillamook. There was a blimp base in Tillamook, and when the surrender came, everything broke loose! There was a big dance at the local hall and a lot of blimp pilots came—it was wild! I was fifteen at the time—so it was all very interesting. It was also the first time I had ever seen contact lens put in someone's eyes! The girl was in the rest room trying to put them back in and they looked so uncomfortable! They were made to fit over the eyeball in those days! I said, "No way will I ever wear those things!" And I didn't!

High School in Bend

All during this time, Mary Jean and I were going to school in Bend. I was going through high school and Mary Jean through grade school. She and I boarded with different people in Bend during the hard part of the winter sometimes. I know I stayed with Connie Tyson, as did Mary Jean, during my sophomore year. It made it easier to attend class events and games! I was on the run all the time, I think! I know this was the year I met my first real boyfriend, Don, but we only went together for about two months. Then we broke up over some slight, with hurt feelings on both sides, but our friendship survived. A few years ago I saw him for the first time after many, many years, and we had a lot of fun playing catch up! He had been in the Air Force during the war, was a pilot and came back, and retired and returned to Bend. He was killed about twelve years ago by a renegade Indian family who were camped next to him in Southern Oregon while he fished. They shot him in the back and died there. His son came down that night and found him. It was quite a story in Oregon at the time. They caught the family and I have the whole story in my files. He left a nice family in Bend.

High school was a lot of fun and I kept real busy during those years. My best friend was Roma and we still see each other. She lives in Idaho. We were together all the time. I stayed with her and she stayed with me! We were good friends with everyone but neither of us wanted to join a "clique"—we just wanted to be on our own. And we were! We had fun with everyone. We had some classes together and we would meet for lunch and after school, if possible. I was a pretty good student and I belonged to a number of organizations such as Girls' Glee, Choir, and the *Lava Bear* paper. I was the business manager for the paper and for the annual named *The Bear Tracks*, so that took up a lot of time each month. First, I would go to all the businesses in downtown Bend and ask for them to give us an ad. Almost all of the businesses would give us an ad. The cost was from fifty cents to two dollars. Then, after the ad ran, I had to go back and collect the money for each ad. I got out of school in the afternoon to do that with a special permission slip. I ran for student-body secretary one year and lost! But that didn't matter, for I still was into everything I enjoyed.

The last part of my junior year and until January of my senior year, I went with Ray. His family lived near where Aunt Dorothy and Uncle Bill lived in Bend. His dad worked at the Brooks Scanlon mill, and we had to go pick him up at midnight when he worked nights. Ray and I were close friends and then he went into the service. He was stationed at Fort Lewis here in Tacoma. He would get leave every two or three weeks and hitchhike to Bend for two or three days.

One time, Claude and I drove to Maupin and picked him up after he called and said he could get a ride that far. After his visit, he had to go back to Fort Lewis and, if he was late, he had to mop floors! He and I had dates that were mostly going out with his gun, a 30-06, and with my .22 rifle. We would go over to Big River, up to LaPine, and any place we could find a place to shoot at limbs and tin cans. I shot his gun once—that was enough! It had a kick to it like a mule! I stuck with my .22 and had a great time. We went together until January of 1947. Then, because I was in my senior year, I wanted to be free to go out with friends

Gracie and Barbara

without him worrying about it, and he agreed with me. We stayed friends and I saw him once in Bend about twenty years ago and we had dinner and talked over old times! I believe it was a more innocent time in those early days in Bend, but I wouldn't have traded that time for anything! There are still a number of the people I grew up with that I see once a year at a LaPine/Shevlin reunion, and we do have a great time. Most of them had come to the ranch as children with their parents or had gone to the swimming hole at the north end of the ranch to swim.

Jobs

I graduated from Bend High School in May of 1947. I had had a part-time job at Montgomery Wards after school and on weekends up until then. I made the large sum of 50 cents an hour! A friend of Claude's, Vern Larson, asked me to come and see him after graduation. He had an insurance agency, and I went to work for him and stayed about a year. Then I went to Lumberman's Insurance Agency, which is still a large agency in Bend, and worked there, typing policies—had to put all the details in ourselves—and from there, I went to the Pacific Tel & Tel as a telephone operator.

I loved that job, even with

Gracie Vandevert

106

the crazy hours that I worked. This was the day when we only had one telephone company and we called it "Ma Bell." It also was the time when, as operators, we would have a headset on and plug into a board and sit down for our day's work. A light would come on the board, and we would plug into it and say, "Number, please." The party would just give us a number, such as 251, and we would put the plug into that number and ring the phone manually. The phones, at that time, had no dial of any kind. You simply picked it up and asked the operator for your number. Also, if there were a fire emergency in town, the volunteer firemen would call in and ask us where the fire was. The board would really light up, and we had to work extra fast to give out the details to the fireman calling us. I started out with split shifts, such as four hours in the morning and four in late afternoon or evening. I finally worked up my seniority to choose my hours, and I then worked from 6:00 A.M. until 3:00 P.M. I liked that shift—still had a lot of the day left! I worked there two years.

Tom McNellis

Right after I graduated, I met Tom McNellis! He was born in Philadelphia, Pennsylvania, and grew up across the Delaware River in New Jersey. He had come to California and Oregon and had landed in Bend. He was working at the Fall River Fish Hatchery just past the ranch. I met him the day after my eighteenth birthday—July 5—as I had gone to an airshow with one of his co-workers, Glen Garrison. The next week Glen called to tell me that Tom had cut his foot badly and was in St. Charles Hospital in Bend. I laughingly said, "I'll have to go see him!" and Glen said, "Yes, you should, as he is new here and

Tom and Gracie

hasn't any friends nearby!" So, I trotted up to the hospital—couldn't remember his last name and asked to see a fellow named Tom who had cut his foot open! They sent me back to the men's ward, and there he was with two women standing by the bed! I walked back—not knowing what to expect, and he seemed genuinely glad to see me. Turned out the two ladies were Glen's mother and her friend who were bringing him some things he needed.

I continued to visit with him twice a day until he was released and then we started going together. Tom worked at the hatchery and also the Pacific Power & Light Co. in Bend. He also tried working for two or three months near Shelton, Washington, at Camp Grisdale in the woods. The rain finally drove him back to Bend. Soon after that, he went to work at the Trailway Bus Depot as a ticket agent. His boss was Bill Crooks. That is where we made a lot of friends who are still in Bend to this day. We had a lot of fun times and were married in February 1950 in Klamath Falls, Oregon. We were married by a Judge Mahoney who was the father of twelve (!) children, six boys and six girls! We saw the pictures of them!

Back in Bend, Tom's mother and sister, Mary Jane, were living with him at the time, so we were one big happy family those first few months. Then, they went back to Philadelphia and Tom and I stayed with Uncle Bill and Aunt Dorothy for a couple months while Uncle Bill recovered from some surgery. Aunt Dorothy was working at St. Charles Hospital and I was pregnant, so it all worked out fine. I had quit my job, and after taking care of Uncle Bill, we got a small, one-bedroom house on the west side of Bend.

Son Tom

Tom was working for Lundgren at this time, and on April 11, 1951, our first son, Tom, was born, with my Uncle Doc doing the delivery. I also had several friends who were nurses there. One who cared for me was Ann Grunfelder. She was an old friend of the family and she was an anesthetist for the hospital. She and her sister, Emma, lived a block from the hospital in an apartment. Neither was married and they took turns at the hospital, as Emma was also an anesthetist. When I was very young, my mother would leave me with them for a couple hours when we came to town. They would let me take a real bath in a real bathtub with bubble bath! It was quite exciting! I really hated being away from my mother, but I usually was okay when with them. So, it was wonderful having them there to urge me on with my first son.

Philadelphia

Around the end of May that year, Tom came home from work one evening and said, "Let's go back to Philadelphia." After my initial shock, I said, "Okay!" He wanted to finish his tool & die/machinist trade that he had started in trade school. We took all our belongings to my dad at the ranch, and he left for the East Coast. I moved in with Dad and stayed there about three weeks. I packed all the things we would need into a large trunk from the ranch and it was shipped ahead of us to Philadelphia.

Tom got a job at Leeds and Northrop in Philadelphia and told me to come on back. I tried to get an airplane ticket—they were on strike! I waited and waited, and finally my dad suggested I go by train. He helped me get a "roomette" on the train and saw me off in Bend on the bus to The Dallas, where I caught the train that evening. Here I was with a tiny baby and leaving all that I had grown up with. I spent three nights and two long days on that train. I can only remember how I just sat there watching the countryside go by and wondering what was ahead. I tried to take Tommy with me up to the dining car and just couldn't handle the swaying of the train. I got very hungry. The porter finally saw my plight, and he actually baby-sat with Tommy while I went to have a big dinner.

I got to Chicago and that same porter saw to it that I knew just where to go and actually watched over me until I left almost three hours later. I have never forgotten that kindness. I then found that on the overnight trip into Philadelphia I could just ring a buzzer and they would bring my meal to me. That was a delight—and then the porter made up a bottom bunk for me and I actually slept good going into Philadelphia. We arrived at 6:00 A.M., and Tom was there with a cab to take us home.

We stayed with Aunt Margaret McKibben for a couple of weeks and then moved in with Mom McNellis and Aunt Ethel Thomas in the Abbottsford project near East Falls. When I arrived in Philadelphia, I felt so hot and sticky. Tom said it was the humidity. We went shopping right away so I could buy cotton dresses to wear instead of the woolen things I had brought from Bend. Very few people had air-conditioning at that time—so cotton was a welcome relief.

The first day I was in Philadelphia Tom and I walked down Germantown Avenue to shop, and he took me into a small pub with just a counter. He asked me to look up on the wall of pub and that is where I saw my first television set. It was black and white, and it had a commercial on advertising Esslinger's beer! I have never forgotten that moment. Quite a fascinating thing to see for the first time.

While we lived in Philadelphia, we got to visit a lot of historical places and also had lots of trips to New Jersey. We went over there to go swimming in the lakes! It was very hot and humid in the summers there and really cold and damp in the winter. We also had a great trip to Canada the last summer we lived there. We drove to Niagara Falls and then up to Fenlon Falls, Ontario, where Mom McNellis was born. We took both Mom and Aunt Ethel with us. We stayed for a few days on a large lake in Algonquin Provincial Park. We fished and just relaxed and talked to the wonderful Canadian people. Then we went back across Lake Champlain into New York and down through the New England states and back to Philadelphia. I always thought that Philadelphia was a beautiful city. It had the longest park within a city in the world. Except for the humid weather and cold in the winter, I enjoyed my time there and learned there was a whole world out there a long ways from the ranch.

While living in Philly, I worked at the Home Insurance Company right across the street from Independence Hall. I rode a small bus from our apartment down to Broad and Erie Avenue. Then I rode the subway down to about Sixth and Market Street, and from there I walked to work. I was on the fifth floor of the Public Ledger building, which was right next to Curtis Publishing Company. I could look out our window and see the *Saturday Evening Post* running off on the presses right across from us. At lunchtime, I would go over to the Independence Mall square and eat and enjoy looking at that Hall. At that time the bell was still inside, but now they have taken it to a mall in front. I could buy a hot pretzel with mustard and make lunch out it! They were so big! I had good friends there and only worked about six months when I had to leave as I was pregnant with Mike. That summer we drove to the Pocono Mountains in upstate Pennsylvania for a week.

Son Mike

By this time we had moved to a second-story apartment close to Temple University Hospital off Broad Street. We were living there when Mike was born on September 17, 1952. We had five different nationality doctors who helped me through that delivery. A Dr. Ho delivered Mike. A black doctor stayed with me through all my labor, and I have never forgotten that. We had a Jewish doctor, a German doctor and an Italian doctor, so I was introduced to a whole new world away from Bend. Mary Jane came and took care of Tommy, and I remember that Aunt Sadie came to see us in the hospital and brought Mike a whole new outfit to wear home. Tom's father, Tom McNellis Sr., died in October. He got to see two of his grandchildren, and I had always hoped he would be able to come to visit us in the West.

I have always told people that my experience in Philadelphia was wonderful. I was terribly homesick, but I felt so privileged to have seen so many historic places that I might have missed. I loved the restaurants there. I found the Jewish delicatessens and the wonderful German bakeries—also the fabulous candies made there. And the cheesecake in Philly was to die for. It was so good! I was also introduced to scrapple, a Philly specialty meat that could be used for breakfast, lunch or supper. It was inexpensive and I liked it. There were Automat cafes there in those days. You could put a nickel in a slot and get a cup of coffee and put in a dime and get a piece of pie. It was a great place to stop when in a hurry. There were also the diners made like railroad cars all over the town. We had a couple favorites that we went to near where we lived. You could always depend on their food—always good. One other favorite thing I saw in Philly was the annual New Year's Day parade called the Mummers' parade. It consisted of just string bands and it was wonderful. There were probably thirty to thirty-five bands, and we would sit through all of them parading up Broad Street.

We took one trip to New York City and, to me, that was enough! We saw Grant's Tomb, walked down Fifth Avenue, and went up in the Empire State Building. I found the whole place overwhelming! I was glad to get back to Philly! This was in 1953 when the boys were still small. We decided that the following year we would go back to Oregon. So, we made plans and, in the meantime, my sister, Mary Jean, came back and lived with us for a year.

When we were ready to go back, we piled everything in the car and headed west. We stopped to see Aunt Martha and Uncle Bush in Sellersburg, Indiana, and stayed with them two nights. Then, on we went west! We broke down in Soda Springs, Idaho, got it fixed, broke down again, got it fixed, made it to Boise, and it happened again! Some fun! Our money was running out by then! But we finally made it to Bend. I was never so glad to see a place as I was that Pilot Butte! Now I know how the pioneers felt who were going out West! We stopped at Claude and Nancy's and then went to the ranch.

Jeanie Jossey Vandevert

While we were in Philadelphia, Dad had met Jeanie Jossey of Newburg, Oregon. She was visiting her sister-in-law at the Spring River Resort, which is just a mile from the bridge by Sun River. My sister, Mary Jean, was working there in the little café, and when Dad stopped by to see her, Mary introduced Jeanie and Dad. Well, that relationship ended up in a wonderful marriage. Both were widowed, and they lived the first winter in the old log house. Jeanie was a good sport about that, but they decided to build a new modern home. This they did in late 1953 and was where they were living when we arrived back from Philadelphia. Jeanie and I were already friends, as we had talked and written to each other. She was a wonderful, giving, and caring woman, and my dad was very lucky to have found another wonderful woman for the last half of his life. After Dad died in 1975, I visited Jeanie as often as possible, and we were always great friends.

My Father Claude and Jeanie

Gig Harbor

Tom left for Portland to look for a job in his field as a tool & die maker/machinist, and I stayed with Dad and Jeanie. I was seven months pregnant and wanted to get settled soon. Tom called from Portland and said he was going to look in the Seattle area—Dad told him that our old friend, Bill Routley, was in Gig Harbor, Washington. Tom found Bill, who was working for the Puget Sound Naval Shipyard in Bremerton, and decided to try to get on. Well, he did, on the day he applied. He worked for a week, came back to the ranch, picked us up, and took us to Gig Harbor! This was in the latter part of May 1954, and when we came across the Narrows Bridge, I thought it was the end of the world! Couldn't see any homes with all those trees! I soon got used to them and the beautiful area. It wasn't too different from Oregon except it rained more and the trees were in abundance with loads of underbrush!

Son John

We rented a small home near Bill and Doris Routley of Gig Harbor, and on July 15, 1954, we had John at Tacoma General Hospital in Tacoma. Dr. Bogue delivered John, and he was my doctor for my next two boys. We moved to Wauna for the winter but had seen a house that we liked in the Point Fosdick area. We finally bought the house in 1955 and moved in September. It was a wonderful big house with four bedrooms and two baths! It was like heaven after living in small, one-bedroom rentals!

Son Steve

That December 2, 1955, we had our number four son, Steve, and Grandma McNellis was living with us at the time. I was given a baby shower by some neighbors and had new things to start his life. There were a lot of hand-me-downs in those days! Right after

Christmas, Gramma McNellis got word that her youngest daughter, Dolores, had died. She left the next day for Philadelphia.

Son Joe

We settled into our great home and, on February 2, 1958, we had our fifth son, Joe! Dr. Bogue, and also Dr. Lambing, delivered him. Both were in attendance for Steve and Joe. Dr. Lambing had been in the service when we first came to Gig Harbor. So, I was lucky to have two very capable doctors to take care of me! Dr. Bogue was afraid to come in to see me after Joe's birth—thought I would be upset with another boy! Well, I surely put his mind to rest in a hurry! Already had his name picked out! Tom and I both were happy with our boys! In future years, they have given us lots of girls, to make it a little more even in the family! Their Grandfather Claude thought they were the greatest things since sliced bread! Of course, he felt that way about all his grandkids! My big regret is that they never knew their Grandmother Pearl. She would have loved them all to death!

My Sons, L-R: Tom, Steve, Mike, Joe, and John

The End of an Era—1975

Grace Vandevert McNellis

Claude Jr., Mary Jean, Claude Sr., Gracie, and Dave

This is the just about the end of this story and the end of an era. But I just wanted to give you an idea of my life growing up on the Vandevert Ranch, because you just don't find that type of life anymore! We had no microwaves, televisions, blenders, frozen dinners, saran wrap, foil, ball point pens, credit cards, and a hundred other things that are too numerous to put down! And we didn't have running water, electricity, or a lot of money, but, in looking back, we had "the best of times and the worst of times" with many changes over those years. We had colds, measles, mumps, chicken pox, and other diseases.

It was a hard, tough life to keep that ranch going, and money could be scarce at times. Somehow, through perseverance, my folks kept it going and left us a heritage of hard work, loads of fun, love of family, and a life that I wouldn't have traded for anything in the world. I have always thought that I was the luckiest girl in the world to have been born when I was, to the parents I had, and that they gave me the start in life that has followed me all my days. For that, I will ever be grateful!

I must remember to tell you that my dad thought the Sun River Development was just great, and he liked what they did with the property. He helped them name the streets in Sun River and gave them general information about the area. For this, in later years, they named one of the banquet rooms in his honor. He thought that was rather special.

The ranch was purchased in 1987 by Jim and Carol Gardner. Since then Jim has been writing a book, titled *I Spied a Young Cowboy*, about the history of the Vandevert Ranch.

Since writing this journal, Claude and I have decided that any papers of value regarding the family will be given to the High Desert Museum for safekeeping. Claude and I feel that this is the best place for all the documents, as they will be archived and taken care of for the future.

The first cousins, L-R: Allen, Kathyrn, Vincent, Joan, Dave, Cynthia, Sallie Bird, Claude, Grace, and Barbara (Family Reunion, 1992, near the ranch.)

Grace McNellis
(253) 858-7420
P.O. Box 1524
Gig Harbor, WA 98335

Email—grace7429@aol.com

Purchase Order

DATE	P.O. NO.

CUSTOMER	SHIP TO

ITEM	DESCRIPTION	QTY	PRICE	AMOUNT
Book 40-X	*Home on the Vandevert Ranch* Grace McNellis 1-880222-40-X		14.95	
	Sales Tax (WA residents, 8%)			
	Shipping and handling: 1-2 books $2.00, 3-4 $2.50, 4-5 $3.00, 6-9 $3.50, 10+ $4.00			
		TOTAL		

 RED APPLE PUBLISHING 15010 - 113TH ST. KPN • GIG HARBOR, WA 98329-5014 • FAX (253) 884-1451
PHONE (253) 884-1450 OR (877) 884-1450 • EMAIL peggy@redapplepublishing.com